Deborah Gohrke

The Role of Hope in Leadership

To Michael —

A smart, perceptive, creative student and a fantastic human being.

With gratitude,

Deb

Deborah Gohrke

The Role of Hope in Leadership

VDM Verlag Dr. Müller

Impressum/Imprint (nur für Deutschland/ only for Germany)

Bibliografische Information der Deutschen Nationalbibliothek: Die Deutsche Nationalbibliothek verzeichnet diese Publikation in der Deutschen Nationalbibliografie; detaillierte bibliografische Daten sind im Internet über http://dnb.d-nb.de abrufbar.

Alle in diesem Buch genannten Marken und Produktnamen unterliegen warenzeichen-, marken- oder patentrechtlichem Schutz bzw. sind Warenzeichen oder eingetragene Warenzeichen der jeweiligen Inhaber. Die Wiedergabe von Marken, Produktnamen, Gebrauchsnamen, Handelsnamen, Warenbezeichnungen u.s.w. in diesem Werk berechtigt auch ohne besondere Kennzeichnung nicht zu der Annahme, dass solche Namen im Sinne der Warenzeichen- und Markenschutzgesetzgebung als frei zu betrachten wären und daher von jedermann benutzt werden dürften.

Coverbild: www.purestockx.com

Verlag: VDM Verlag Dr. Müller Aktiengesellschaft & Co. KG
Dudweiler Landstr. 99, 66123 Saarbrücken, Deutschland
Telefon +49 681 9100-698, Telefax +49 681 9100-988, Email: info@vdm-verlag.de
Zugl.: Seattle, Seattle University, Diss., 2007

Herstellung in Deutschland:
Schaltungsdienst Lange o.H.G., Berlin
Books on Demand GmbH, Norderstedt
Reha GmbH, Saarbrücken
Amazon Distribution GmbH, Leipzig
ISBN: 978-3-639-02272-8

Imprint (only for USA, GB)

Bibliographic information published by the Deutsche Nationalbibliothek: The Deutsche Nationalbibliothek lists this publication in the Deutsche Nationalbibliografie; detailed bibliographic data are available in the Internet at http://dnb.d-nb.de.

Any brand names and product names mentioned in this book are subject to trademark, brand or patent protection and are trademarks or registered trademarks of their respective holders. The use of brand names, product names, common names, trade names, product descriptions etc. even without a particular marking in this works is in no way to be construed to mean that such names may be regarded as unrestricted in respect of trademark and brand protection legislation and could thus be used by anyone.

Cover image: www.purestockx.com

Publisher:
VDM Verlag Dr. Müller Aktiengesellschaft & Co. KG
Dudweiler Landstr. 99, 66123 Saarbrücken, Germany
Phone +49 681 9100-698, Fax +49 681 9100-988, Email: info@vdm-publishing.com

Printed in the U.S.A.
Printed in the U.K. by (see last page)
ISBN: 978-3-639-02272-8

ACKNOWLEDGEMENT

Thank you to Amos, Amynomeme, and Athena.

If better leadership role models exist, I don't who they are.

TABLE OF CONTENTS

Acknowledgements 5

Chapter One - Introduction to the Study 10

Background.. 11

Statement of the Problem 12

Purpose of the Study 14

Theoretical Framework 15

Hope Theory 16

Research Question 17

Definition of Key Terms 18

Significance of the Study 20

Limitations of the Study.. 21

Organization of the Study 22

Chapter Two - Review of the Literature............................ 23

Brief History and General Introduction to Hope 23

Hope's Origin in Greek Mythology 24

Hope in Theology and Philosophy........................... 25

Hope and Psychology 30

Hope Compared to Optimism 32

Snyder's Hope Theory.. 34

Goals... 35

Waypower (Pathways thinking)........................... 35

Willpower (Agency thinking) 35

Hope and Health Care.. 36

Section Summary 38

Nonprofit Organizations and Leadership 39

Nonprofits Compared to Other Organizations.......... 39

   Motivation.. 40

Role of the Nonprofit CEO or Executive Director ... 43

An Organizational Model 45

Section Summary 48

Hope and Leadership... 49

Philosophical Framework 50

Complexity of Leadership 51

   Leadership as Relationship 51

   Leadership and Conflict...................................... 52

   Responsibility, Meaning and Hope 53

   Leadership as Activity 54

   The Role of Followers 55

   Honesty, Trust and Hope 56

   Trust and Servant Leadership 57

   Trust and Social Justice 58

   New Metaphors for Leadership........................... 62

Snyder's Hope Theory and Leadership 63

   Goals.. 64

      Warning Signs: Anger and Apathy 65

      Burnout and Goals... 66

      Autonomy and Goals 67

      Leadership Processes & Hope Processes........ 68

Suggested Functions of Hope in Leadership 70

   Reclaiming Hope... 70

   The Dark Side of Hope 72

Section Summary 73

Chapter Three - Research Design and Method 75

    Design 75

    Data 75

        Data Collection 77

        Data Analysis 77

    Methodological Assumptions 80

    Researcher's Bias 81

Chapter Four – Presentation and Analysis of Data 83

    The Data Collecting Experience 83

    Similarities Among Participants 85

Introduction of Participants 86

        Amos the Prophet 87

        Amynomeme the Defender 89

        Athena the Communitarian 91

    Presentation of Findings 93

        Personal Values 94

        Education 98

        Justice and Social Justice 101

        Fear, Faith and Courage 108

        Authenticity 115

            Purpose 116

            Freedom and Responsibility 117

            Truth 120

        Mission 122

        Social Capital 125

        Leadership 128

        Leadership and Hope 131

Summary and Conclusion...................................... 132

Conceptual Framework..................................... 134

Theoretical Framework.................................... 135

Finding Hope... 136

Chapter Five – Conclusions and Recommendations......... 137

Summary of Findings 137

What Did Not Work 139

What Did Worked 140

Conclusions.. 141

Virtue 142

Limitations of the Study 145

Recommendations for Policy................................. 146

Recommendations for Future Research.................. 147

Concluding Thoughts 148

References   152

CHAPTER ONE

INTRODUCTION TO THE STUDY

A jury convicted Ken Lay on all counts, but long before the jury reached its verdict the court of public opinion found the former CEO of Enron guilty of gross failure of leadership (McLean & Elkind, 2003). In the wake of leadership disasters at Adelphia, Enron, Global Crossing, Imclone, Tyco, WorldCom and other organizations, interest has grown in what makes a good leader today. Colleges and universities have rushed to add courses on ethics and adopt new leadership studies programs in response to public outrage over egregious breaches of ethical behavior on the part of many leaders (Educational Directories Unlimited, 2006). Although some business leaders may attribute corporate scandals to a few unethical executives, Yankelovich and Rosell (2006) stated, "A 2002 Gallup Poll found that almost 80 percent of the public believes corruption is endemic in the corporate world and that executive greed and immorality are the top causes of current economic woes." In government, corruptive and unethical behaviors are so common a Washington reporter referred to the 2006 rash of congressional scandals as "blatant, numbskull corruption" (Jenks, 2006). Unfortunately, distrust in leaders has become widespread throughout the public and private sectors, even spreading to the nonprofit sector. Leaders of nonprofit organizations have failed their fiduciary responsibility so often that charity watchdogs have made a business of routinely exposing "non-for-profit profiteers" and "charity chiselers" (Crowley, 2006). This prevalence of crooks and incompetents in positions of leadership has fostered so much widespread cynicism that comedian Lily Tomlin quipped, "No matter how cynical you get, it is impossible to keep up" (thequotationpage.com, 2006). News stories of overpaid executives, golden parachutes, and leaders who have absconded with millions of dollars have become commonplace. And then there are the bumbling, ineffective leaders that rarely make the front-page news, who instead inspire comic strips (e.g., Dilbert) and television comedies (e.g., The Office) that, although funny, are often painfully close to reality. Whether it is leadership that is unethical or ineffective, we are inundated with examples of bad leadership. However, interest in what makes a good or bad leader is not new. Bass (1990) noted, "leadership is one of the world's oldest preoccupations," (p. 3). Leadership and hope are the focus of this study.

Background

Researchers have advanced many different categories of leadership theories: great-man, trait, situational, psychoanalytic, humanistic, contingency, transactional, and transformational (Bass, 1990; Yukl, 2002). More than forty leadership theories are described in *The Encyclopedia of Leadership* (Burns, Goethals & Sorenson, 2004) and more than 225 definitions of leadership are found in the professional literature (Kouzes & Posner 2006). Additionally, interest in the role that followers play in relation to leaders is growing. Research has shown that unconscious desires and behaviors of followers may contribute to the toxic behavior of leaders (Heifetz, 1994; Kellerman, 2004; & Lipman-Blumen, 2005) and that followers who abdicate personal responsibility or fail to oppose unethical leadership invite leaders to act recklessly (Gardner, 1987; Koestenbaum & Block, 2001). But what *is* leadership?

Heifetz (1994) argued that leadership should be viewed as an activity rather than as the province of a person or a position, "the activity of a citizen from any walk of life mobilizing people to do something" (p. 20.). On the other hand, individuals who occupy certain positions, such as a chief executive officer

11

or executive director, are expected to lead. But having a leadership position and leading effectively or ethically is far from assured.

Although scholars have come a long way in developing models of ethical and effective leadership (Barnard 1968; Bass, 1990; Burns et al., 2004), applications of that leadership knowledge are often missing in organizations. There are still gaps in our knowledge of leadership. This study suggests that one of those gaps is in the area of tacit knowledge, something that is so obvious it is given little thought and, therefore, never made explicit. Something that is critical for maximizing the potential of what organizations often claim is their most valuable resource–people.

Statement of the Problem

"The first and last task of a leader is to keep hope alive," according to John W. Gardner (1968, p. 134). If keeping hope alive is the alpha and omega of leadership, we ought to know something about hope and how it is kept alive. How do leaders *do* hope? Hope is an obscure concept that is largely missing in leadership studies. In the encyclopedic *Bass and Stogill's Handbook of Leadership* (1990), hope is not mentioned in the table of contents and is missing from the subject index. Although the concept of hope is implicit in many leadership theories it is rarely the focus. When hope is mentioned, it is understood more as a platitude rather than the cornerstone of good leadership. Hope apparently needs no explanation. But how much do leaders really understand about the nature and function of hope in relation to leadership performance?

While hope has long been a subject of theology and philosophy, research in psychology has demonstrated that hope is a powerful tool that may be developed in order to help individuals function optimally (Cheavens, Michael,

& Snyder, 2005). Research in psychology has discovered much about the nature of hope, its essential components, and the critical role it plays in motivation for accomplishing tasks and achieving goals.

Martin Seligman (1990), professor of psychology and a past president of the American Psychological Association, was uneasy about psychology's fixation on the disease model and suggested more attention be paid to the development of a preventative or health model that focused on building positive strengths. The resulting shift in focus has been dubbed positive psychology. Within the positive psychology movement, hope is viewed as a *learned* trait (Snyder, McDermott, Cook & Rapoff, 1997), which research has shown may be intentionally fostered in children in order to help them become capable and productive adults (Snyder et al., 1997). Although the foundation for developing individual hope occurs during infancy, especially with the development of "basic trust," adults must find sufficient reason to hope from within a larger sociological context to thrive (Erikson, 1959, p. 55). Furthermore, studies on hope have shown that a causal relationship exists between our psychological state and our biological state (Cousins, 1989; Farran, Herth & Popovich, 1995). The implications for improving individual health and subjective well-being through the intentional cultivation of hope are too significant to ignore. Perhaps nowhere does the deliberate cultivation of hope hold more promise than in the development of a collective will to achieve a common vision.

Leaders do not exist except in the context of accomplishing a group purpose, argued Gardner (1990). Leadership scholar Jean Lipman-Blumen asked, "Leadership for what?" (Personal communication, November 19, 2005). Assuming groups and organizations share some common interest(s), the first and last task of leadership is to keep hope alive so that common interests may be served or a common purpose accomplished.

History provides many examples of leaders who inspired the hopes and marshaled the efforts of others to accomplish a common purpose during extraordinary circumstances. Leadership in mundane circumstances may be more difficult. Day-to-day hope is needed in order to grow, adapt to change, face new challenges and accomplish goals. Organizational leadership studies have largely ignored how hope actually functions, or does not function, within the performance of leadership. Why?

The statement, "the first and last task of a leader is to keep hope alive," (Gardner, 1968, p. 134.) contains two assumptions: (a) leaders are in some way responsible for the hope of others, and (b) leaders are capable of keeping hope alive or allowing it to die. If true, in which ways, and to what extent, are leaders responsible for the hope of others? How do leaders perceive and fulfill this responsibility? How does hope actually function in the performance of leadership? How can the implicit uses of hope in leadership become more explicit?

Purpose of the Study

The purpose of the study was to develop a better understanding of how hope functions in the performance of leadership. The context of the study was nonprofit organizations and the participants were executive directors or chief executive officers. The goal of the study was to discover how hope functions in the performance of leadership by leaders of nonprofit organizations in order to make the tacit functions of hope more explicit.

Theoretical Framework

The broadest theoretical underpinning came from existential themes described by the theoretical perspectives on hope outlined in *Hope and Hopelessness: Critical Clinical Constructs* (Farran, Herth, & Popovich, 1995). These authors suggested that the experiential, spiritual, relational and rational attributes of hope are supported by existential literature from psychology, philosophy, and theology. Existential themes such as suffering, despair, death, freedom and accountability are related to finding hope and meaning. Frankl (1984) referred to the human journey as "man's search for meaning" and concluded, "if there is meaning in life at all, then there must be meaning in suffering" (p. 76). Furthermore, it is episodes of anxiety, suffering and despair that most clarify hope (Marcel, 1962).

An existential perspective views people as more than biologically determined organisms. With the exception of persons with rare developmental and biological disorders, people possess both the freedom and the responsibility to choose how they respond to life's circumstances. The philosophical underpinnings of this study will be developed in the review of literature under hope and leadership.

Hope Theory

Hope Theory (Snyder, 2002), a cognitive model of hope, was chosen as a theoretical guide for this study for its pragmatism. It operationalizes hope in a way that allows it to be identified in the performance of leadership more easily than abstract theories of hope. Theoretically, by addressing the distinct elements within Hope Theory, it is possible to analyze evidence of hope, or lack of hope, in a variety of circumstances (Cheaven, Michael, & Snyder, 2005). Snyder stated, *"Hope is the sum of perceived capabilities to produce routes to desired goals, along with the perceived motivation to use those routes"* (italics original, Snyder, 2000a, p. 8). This is a refined version of an earlier definition in which hope is described as *clearly defined goals*, plus *waypower thinking* (agency or the ability to determine pathways to reach those goals) and *willpower thinking* (the motivation to pursue those goals) (Snyder, 1994; Snyder, McDermott, Cook, & Rapoff, 1997). Hope, then, is like a three legged stool—goals + willpower + waypower. Theoretically, with a little investigation, a leader could identify which leg of the stool was wobbly, in a less than hopeful situation within their organization, and then work to strengthen that leg.

For example, I began this study with the very broad goal of understanding hope, which proved to be a problem for developing high hope of ever finishing the study. To strengthen the goal leg of my theoretical, three legged stool, I needed to identify a more *specific* goal in relation to the study of hope. Once my goal became clear, I found that I needed *more* waypower (agency thinking—the ability to identify effective pathways to achieve the goal). I had plenty for willpower (motivation), but willpower alone would not be enough. As for the axiom, "Where there's a will there is a way," Snyder (1994) confirmed that this is not always the case. His research has consistently supported the idea that persons with willpower thinking do not always have waypower thoughts. "If the person does not have both the willpower and waypower for goals, there cannot be high hope. Put in another way, neither willpower or waypower alone is sufficient to produce high hope" (Snyder, 1994, p.10). New learning, along with the guidance of others who did have high waypower thinking, enabled me to increase my hope in respect to this study. As a result I narrowed the goal and identified new pathways in which I would be able to reach it. Although this description is a simplification and reduction of the entire process that I experienced; conceptualizing hope in this way *works*.

> We always have choices about the level of abstraction at which to conceptualize and talk about things, ranging from the very concrete…to the very abstract, where many different things are grouped in a way that homogenizes them and focuses on a few characteristics they have in common at the expense of a focus on differences. (Foss & Waters, 2007)

Choosing to conceptualize hope less abstractly does not capture the relational, iterative and dynamic *process* of hoping. However, it illustrates a basic structure of hope and suggests three distinct areas for how to develop self-hope, foster hope in others, and apply it in specific situations.

Research Question

The purpose of this study was to develop a better understanding of how hope functions in the performance of leadership. The leadership context was from within an organization and from the perspective of participants who served in a position from which others expected leadership. This research question guided the study: How does hope function in the performance of leadership among leaders of nonprofit organizations?

Definition of Key Terms

Practical definitions that lend themselves to observation have been selected for this study; however, hope and leadership are abstract concepts. Leadership occurs in the human mind and is not a tangible event that can be studied scientifically (Harter, 2006). Hope, likewise, cannot be systematically dissected in a laboratory. Scholars who study these multifaceted concepts have not agreed on a single definition of hope or leadership. Rather, there are many valid definitions of hope and leadership that serve to enrich one another. These terms will be expanded upon in the review of literature.

Sometimes the best way to define a concept is to begin with its opposite. The opposite of hope is despair. While despair and depression are terms that are sometimes used interchangeably, each has a distinct meaning. Despair is a loss of hope resulting in a sense of futility in pursuing one's goals (Soukhanov, 1992); depression is a low spirit, sadness, or a feeling of despondency that may not be related to an external event. Despair involves *hopelessness;* depression involves *helplessness.* "Depression is a more acute and incapacitating disorder that centers around loss and blame" (Goldsmith, 1987, p. 5). Despair strikes when we care deeply and what we care about is threatened, it reflects unmet longing. Depression, on the other hand, is often characterized by apathy. Depression is not necessarily accompanied by despair, but when both are experienced in combination "they are devastating and suicide is likely to become an urgent question" (Goldsmith, p.5).

Hope and optimism are also words sometimes used interchangeably, although these concepts are distinct. "The optimist has a spectators assurance that things will work out for the best" according to Shade (2001. p. 201). Hopeful persons, in contrast, know that they must participate, that the fate of what is desired depends, in part, upon their contribution. For the sake of clarity, depression and optimism are included among the key terms of this study:

18

despair, hope and leadership. Additional terms that relate to the research question are: function, nonprofit, and executive director.

Depression:

To be depressed means to be *"affected or marked by low spirits"* (Soukhanov, 1992). Depression is often precipitated by the experience of loss and is accompanied by reduced activity and negative thinking. The inability to move forward, or the absence of future pull, is also a characteristic depression shares with despair.

Despair:

Despair means essentially *"to come undone* [se defaire] *in the presence of..."* according to Gabriel Marcel (1951/1996, p.604). For a leader to come undone in the presence of a situation that appears irremediable can paralyze both the leader and the individuals who depend upon the leader to model the way or articulate a strategy. Like depression, despair is marked by reduced activity but it is situational and related to frustrated goals instead of a general feeling of sadness or low spirits. In despair, activity is seen as futile in relation to the achievement of a desired goal or outcome.

Executive Director:

A position held by the person seen as responsible for leading a nonprofit organization in accomplishing its mission. The executive director (ED) may also be referred to as the chief executive officer (CEO) or president, and usually reports to the organization's Board of Directors (Elbert, 2006).

Function:

"The special kind of activity proper to anything; the mode of action which fulfils its purpose" (Oxford English Dictionary, 2002). In this study, function is the underlying purpose for the use of hope by the participants in the performance of leadership.

Hope:

"Hope is the sum of perceived capabilities to produce routes to desired goals, along with the perceived motivation to use those routes" (italics original, Snyder, 2000a, p. 8).

Leadership:

Leadership is "the personal capacity for affirming decisions that lend quality and morality to the coordination of organized activity and to the formulation of purpose" (Barnard, 1968, p. vii).

Nonprofit:

A nonprofit is an organization exempt from federal income taxes. The United States Internal Revenue Code defines over 25 categories of organizations exempt from federal income taxes. Nonprofit in this study refers to the category 501(c)(3) of the code that applies to organizations that exist to provide a service for humanity (Elbert, 2006). "Whereas other types of nonprofit organizations benefit the private, social or economic interests of their members, 501(c)(3) nonprofit organizations must benefit the broad public interest" (Independent Sector, 2006).

Optimism:

Optimism is a positive explanatory style in which an individual believes that future events will have a positive outcome (Seligman, 1990). The distinction between hope and optimism is that hope produces behavior directly related to what is hoped for, while optimism is primarily a way of interpreting events.

Significance of the Study

This study helps make the tacit knowledge of the function of hope in the performance of leadership more explicit. Directly relating hope to leadership activities can contribute information to future leadership training programs and can help existing leaders to be better leaders. It helps answer the question of how leaders do (or do not) keep hope alive.

This study benefits nonprofit organizations as it suggests ways in which Chief Executive Officers and Executive Directors may increase their leadership effectiveness, and it contributes to our understanding of how hope functions as it is actually practiced by real people under challenging circumstances who occupy leadership roles.

Limitations of the Study

This study lacks generalizability to a broad population for several reasons. First, the primary purpose of a qualitative phenomenological study is to allow the researcher to gain a deep understanding of the participants' experience, rather than to produce generalizable data. The study was designed to be narrow and deep, limited to a small sample size consisting of 2 chief executive officers and 1 executive director of 3 social service nonprofit organizations. Each leader faced unique challenges. Additionally, their respective organizations are distinct from nonprofits in general, and are particularly distinct from for-profit organizations (Drucker, 1990). Also, the study relied primarily on observations by the researcher who shadowed each participant while they performed their professional duties and was limited by the context and period in time during which the observations occurred. The study relied heavily on the self-report from the participants during in-depth interviews. Other individuals from within their organizations were not asked to verify each participant's perspective. Analysis of written documents augmented the observation and the in-depth interviews. Finally, this study was not longitudinal. It represents a description of specific time frame and does not show the many contextual changes that occur over time and the effect of these changes on the hope and leadership of the participants. Due to these limitations, there may be other ways to conduct a similar study that would add more to our knowledge regarding the function of hope in the performance of leadership.

Organization of the Study

The first chapter introduced the study. Chapter 2 contains a review of the literature on hope and leadership based upon 3 major categories implied by the research question. The categories in the literature review consist of (a) a brief history and general introduction to hope, (b) nonprofit organizations and executive directors, and (c) leadership and hope. Chapter 3 describes the method used to gather data and conduct the study. Chapter 4 consists of a review of the findings. Finally, chapter 5 presents the conclusions and proposes recommendations for leadership policies and future research.

CHAPTER TWO

REVIEW OF THE LITERATURE

We know in our bones that hope is everything.
In the back of our minds, we suspect it is nothing at all.
Maurice Lamm

This is a study about hope and leadership. The review of literature is organized into 3 main sections suggested by the research question: how does hope function in the performance of leadership by leaders of nonprofit organizations? The first section consists of a brief history and general introduction to the philosophical and psychological literature on hope. The second section consists of a brief review of nonprofit organizations and the role of chief executive officers and/or executive directors. Finally, the third section, hope and leadership, reviews the connection between hope and leadership theories, with particular attention paid to research that either stresses the importance of hope or where hope is a logical inference.

Brief History and Introduction to Hope

Martin Luther (1483-1546) observed, "Everything that is done in the world is done by hope." Without hope, why would we even bother to get out of bed in the morning? Hope has a future orientation. It propels us forward. Aside from Nietzsche (1844-1900), who called hope "the worst of all evils," most people see hope as a good thing. But what exactly is hope? How do you know it when you see it? How do you *see* it? Hope is a fuzzy concept that is difficult to articulate and means different things to different people. A dictionary definition of hope is "a wish or desire accompanied by confident expectation of its fulfillment" (Soukhanov, 1992). But this definition belies the complexity of hope. Hope can be general or specific, practical or impractical, natural or supernatural. Hope can be understood as an empowered imagination, a virtue, a gift, a journey, a mystery, or all of above (Lynch, 1965; Pieper, 1997; Marcel, 1962). "Hope is, or can be, positive, negative, divine, secular, interpersonal, individual, social, ideological, inherent, acquired, objective, subjective, a practice, a possession, an emotion, a cognition, true, false, enduring, transitory, measured, defined, inspired, learnt...and the list goes on," according to Eliot (2005, p. 38). In short, hope is a multifaceted construct. But we have gotten ahead of ourselves. How we view hope today has greatly expanded from how hope has been the conceptualized in the past.

Hope's Origin in Greek Mythology

Hope made its first appearance, according to Greek mythology, as an item in Pandora's box (Stewart, 2005). In the struggle of mortal man with the immortal gods, in spite of man's inferior position, the gods were often less noble than man. Prometheus, one of the lesser gods whose name means "foresight," wanted to give humans something they could really use: the gift of fire. But Zeus, a bigger and more powerful god, was less sympathetic towards humans and quashed the idea. Prometheus stole fire from Zeus and gave it to humans anyway. Zeus got so mad that he bound Prometheus to the side of a cliff and let a vulture eat his liver—everyday. Since Prometheus was immortal his liver would grow back overnight in time for breakfast. Zeus wasn't satisfied with this punishment though. He thought he needed to balance the good gift of fire to humans with a gift of his own. He fashioned a beautiful woman named Pandora ("all gifted") and sent her to the brother of Prometheus, Epimetheus ("hindsight"). Epimetheus welcomed Pandora in spite of his brother's warning not to accept any gifts from the gods. Epimetheus, not entirely reckless, told Pandora *never* to open the box she had received from Zeus. Pandora, of course,

24

opens the box and lets out all manner of disease, poverty, crime, suffering—everything bad, (similar to another story in which a woman's curiosity gets the whole world in trouble). When Pandora realized what was happening she quickly closed the lid, leaving one thing in the box—hope. Epimetheus and Pandora hear hope calling to them from the box and figure it can't get any worse so they open the box a second time and hope enters the world, that is according to Stewart's version of this story (2005). You might think if hope was so good what was hope doing hanging out with all that evil? Some people have concluded that hope is really a *bad* thing, "the worst of all evils," according to Nietzsche, because it "prolongs torment" (1844-1900). Which isn't so far-fetched considering the nature of the punishment Zeus devised for Prometheus.

Hope in Theology and Philosophy

Hope is an unavoidable subject of theology and philosophy, as well as a ubiquitous theme in literature. Myths of the hero's journey, as exemplified by Odysseus in Homer's *Odyssey* (1993), are powerful metaphors of hope that imply that there is purpose in our finite human existence and nobility in the search for meaning. The existential philosopher Gabriel Marcel (1962) suggested that the only way for man to achieve stability on earth is to recognize that his condition is that of a traveler. For the human journey, hope is the "only antidote to despair," he claimed in *Homo Viator*, to be a *viator* is to be *on the way*, we are people *on the way* (p. 62). Josef Pieper (1997) referred to hope simply as the *"not yet"* of this pilgrimage, adding that hope is the anticipation of fulfillment, while despair is the anticipation of non-fulfillment (p. 89). For both Marcel and Pieper, hope is equated with more being—more life in the present, as well as a desirable future, the all important *yet* of *not yet*, while despair is simply *not*.

25

Despair and hope are inextricably linked. "The truth is that there can be no hope except when the temptation to despair exists. Hope is the act by which this temptation is actively or victoriously overcome," according to Marcel (1962, p. 36). Paul Tillich (2000) argued hope becomes indistinguishable from courage, the courage to be. In the face of existential doubt, he speaks of an ultimate hope, or a hope that appears when the situation is beyond hope. Immanuel Kant, in *Critique of Pure Reason* (1950), summed up his life's work with three questions: "What can I know? What ought I do? What may I hope?" (p. 635).

Pieper (1969) made a distinction between "hopes" and "hope." Borrowing from the work of Heidelberg physician Herbert Plügge, Pieper argued that, "fundamental" or "genuine" hope has no object that actually exists in the material world (1969, p. 25.). The *something*, which is the object of this hope, is indefinite, nebulous—difficult to describe, in fact, *indescribable* except in analogous language. Ordinary or everyday hope, in contrast, is directed towards "future things pertaining to the world," towards an "object belonging to the world," towards something that comes to us from the outside, which could be a important news or information, an accomplishment, a good relationship or even physical health (1969, p. 26).

However, the distinction between *hope* and *hopes* is not a surgical cut. Phenomenological research has confirmed that there is an iterative relationship between the experience of fundamental hope and everyday hope (Plügge as cited in Pieper, 1969). Fundamental hope is "most convincingly revealed" at the very moment of disappointment, when hopes (plural) collapse and lose their meaning (p. 26). It is at the point during which the situation appears beyond hope that fundamental hope can breathe new life into hopes (plural) or stimulate different hopes (plural), or simply replace hopes (plural) with hope.
The disappointment of our everyday hopes, Pieper claimed, purges "illusory hopes" making way for fundamental hope (p. 26). For example, in the case of a

person who had hoped to beat an advanced stage of cancer and who becomes aware that she will lose the battle to regain her health, "disappointment, then, represents far more than the correction of an erroneous opinion," according to Pieper (p. 26).

> It represents liberation in a sense going far beyond the realm of cognition. Plügge says that possibly the experience of ultimate incurability enables the patient to experience freedom from the imprisonment of illness. Such freedom could not be attained before the collapse [of hopes plural]. (p. 27)

The kind of hope that has nothing to do with what one can *do*, Pieper called "fundamental;" Tillich called "ultimate;" Marcel called "genuine" (Pieper, 1969, Tillich, 2000, Marcel, 1962). Marcel said, "genuine hope is that which is *directed towards something not dependent on ourselves*" (italics mine, Marcel as cited in Pieper, 1969, p. 22).

Nietzsche (1844-1900), on the other hand, claimed hope was the "worst of all evils because it prolongs torment." However, Nietzsche was famous for his self-contradiction. When all of his writing is taken into account, it becomes apparent that when he rails against hope he is actually pleading for it (Atichison, 1996). The same Nietzsche who referred to hope as the worst evil, claimed hope is a "stimulant to life that is much stronger than any realized joy could ever be."

Walter Kaufmann, noted for his highly respected translations of Nietzsche into English, in his prologue to *Thus Spoke Zarathustra,* emphasized Nietzsche is frequently misunderstood and that the single most important "clue to his letters, as also to Zarathustra and some of the last books, is that it is the work of a *thoroughly lonely* man" (italics mine, Nietzsche, 1982, p. xv). Kaufmann's insight on Nietzsche is interesting in light of Marcel's assertion that "hope is always associated with a communion, no matter how interior it may be. This is actually so true that one wonders if despair and solitude are not

27

at bottom necessarily identical" (Marcel, 1962, p. 58). Nietzsche once wrote to a friend, "The barrel of a pistol is for me at the moment a source of relatively agreeable thoughts" (Nietzsche, 1982, p. vx). In the end, the "utterly lonely" Nietzsche was not able to resist despair and died isolated and insane (p. xiii).

Nietzsche was a strong influence on theologians and philosophers, however, who clearly saw hope as one of the greatest of all goods. Marcel (1962), Tillich (2000), Buber (1970), and Frankl (1984), for instance, are all mouthpieces for the power and centrality of hope in a life fully lived. Frankl experienced the truth of Nietzsche's words in the crucible of a Nazi concentration camp, "He who has a *why* to live can bear with almost any *how*" (italics original, Frankl, 1984, p. 84). Hope rests upon *why*, not *how*. It could be paraphrased; he who has hope can bear with any circumstance. Frankl found that "any attempt to restore a man's inner strength in the camp had first to succeed in showing him some future goal" (p. 84). For the prisoner who saw no aim to his life, who lost faith in the future—the future was doomed, and he quickly succumbed to mental and physical decay. Many comrades died of sickness or suicide, but the real reason for their deaths may have been that they gave up hope, suggested Frankl (1984).

Frankl referred to the human journey as "man's search for meaning" and concluded, "If there is meaning in life at all, then there must be meaning in suffering" (1984, p. 76). The goal in life is not to eliminate conflict but rather to act responsibly in the face of the "tragic triad" of pain, guilt and death (p.139). We can choose to say yes to life, to hope. Pain and suffering can be turned into human achievement, guilt can provide the impetus to change oneself for the better, and the awareness of our finite existence can be an incentive to seize the day. Frankl concluded real hope begins by accepting one's freedom and responsibility to find meaning in life. Like cognitive behaviorists, he emphasized the role of individual choice and responsibility, but not for the purpose of maximizing pleasure and avoiding pain. Accepting our freedom and responsibility to choose how we respond to every circumstance in life represents a fundamental change in attitude toward life itself. Under indescribable deprivation Frankl (1984) stated:

> It did not really matter what we expected from life, but rather what life expected from us. We needed to stop asking about the meaning of life and instead to think of ourselves as those who were being questioned by life daily and hourly. (p. 85)

Frankl did not consider hope itself a goal, but saw it as a by-product of a meaningful life. He maintained the unconditional meaningfulness of life could not be grasped in rational terms. Meaning is deeper than logic. While starving, freezing and marching in the dark in a concentration camp, Frankl was transfixed by an epiphany: "The truth—that love is the ultimate and highest goal to which man can aspire....*The salvation of man is through love and in love* " (italics original, p. 49).

Frankl stressed, "The true meaning of life is to be discovered *in* the world rather than within man or his own psyche, as though it were a closed system" (italics mine, 1984, p. 115). The more my existence includes others, according to Marcel, the more I am (1951/1996). "Hope is always centered on a *we*, on a living relationship and if we have not noticed this fact it is because we too often use the word hope when what is at issue is in fact [individual] desire" (p. 608). A fundamental realization is not Descartes' conclusion, I think, therefore I am, but rather *we are*. Lynch argued, "the image of the absolutely self-sufficient man is a mockery of physiological and psychological fact" (1965, p. 44). It is time to step off "Maslow's escalator" in a purely individualistic search for self-actualization (Yankelovich as cited in Bisesi, 1981).

> The search for self-fulfillment cannot succeed unless its seekers discard the assumption of the self as private consciousness, the more private the more real. Only when one understands that the self must be fulfilled within shared meanings of psychoculture is one pursuing self-fulfillment realistically. (p. 648)

It is hope for all of us; hope that goes beyond our individual desire, that elevates us above the brute forces of nature and circumstance and which becomes indistinguishable from love.

Philosophers, theologians, artists and others will always struggle to account for, describe or illustrate the experience of hope; it is an inexhaustible subject, indivisible from life. "Where there's life, there's hope" (Terence, 195-159 BC). But what we observe, logically infer, and operationally define as hope, can never be equated with the phenomenon itself (Valle & Halling, 1989). Rather than a problem to be solved, hope is a mystery to be lived, according to Marcel (1962).

Insights from theologians and philosophers appear throughout this paper with apologies to these authors and the reader for not representing the systematic worldviews in which their thoughts on hope have been developed. However, an arbitrary constraint is essential in the context of this study. An in-depth review of hope literature in theology and philosophy would draw us away from the narrow purpose of the study. For an understanding of hope from three different Western philosophical perspectives see Joseph Godfrey's *The Philosophy of Human Hope* (1987), in which he offers a systematic analysis of hope worked out in dialogue with the writing of Ernst Block (an atheist,) Gabriel Marcel (a Christian theist), and Immanuel Kant (an unconventional theist).

Hope and Psychology

In 1959, Karl Menninger placed hope at the center of psychiatry and medicine in general in a lecture that he delivered to the American Psychiatric Association entitled *Hope* (Eliott, 2005). His lecture is credited with triggering a paradigm shift in the conceptualization of hope within the field of medicine.

Menninger argued inspiring the "right amount of hope—some, but not too much" was the responsibility of the medical practitioner (Menninger as cited in Eliott, 2005, p 11). Two significant concepts took root. The first dealt with the amount of hope—an individual might have an incorrect amount of hope, implying hope could be measured. Second, that the amount of hope an individual possessed could be assessed by medical practitioners who had a responsibility to do something about it. Eliott (2005) argued that with the medicalization of hope, hope became objectified, something that could be passed from person to person. While Menninger borrowed language from existential philosophy and theology to present his conceptualization of hope, the brand of hope he was marketing was definitely rooted in this world. Menninger marketed a hope that was enabling and transformative for the individual in the here and now. Of this objectified hope, Eliot (2005) wrote, "It was individualistic, rather than communal, and was (and is) entirely congruent with the individualistic ethos characteristic of American culture" (p. 12). This new conceptualization of hope is in sharp contrast with the communal nature of philosophic hope in which despair is experienced alone but hope is always experienced in terms of we. Marcel (1962) argued that hope "is always associated with a communion, no matter how interior it may be" (p. 58).

Ezra Stotland (1969) defined hope as "an expectation greater than zero of achieving a goal" (p. 2). He saw hope as a subjective term that could be measured by social scientists. Every measurement of hope carries implicit "assumptions that hope is a possession of the individual, is objectively discernable, can vary, can be altered by judicial intervention, and is a worthwhile attribute to promote" according to Eliot (2004, p. 21). Louis A. Gottschalk's (1974) measurement of hope was the first of many hope measurements. Arguments ensued regarding what was actually being measured, but the processes, the instrumentation and overall predictability of the results convinced many social scientists that the truth about hope could be discovered

31

through empirical research. Yet, in any instrument designed to measure hope, some arbitrary decisions must be made, hope must be simplified. Eliot (2004) argued "the downside of this process of simplification" was that it excluded those aspects of the phenomenon of hope that are not amenable to be measured (p. 17).

Hope shifted from being a mystery to be experienced in communion, to a problem to be solved, to an asset to be developed in the individual. For example, hope viewed as a *virtue* or *character strength,* is something to be identified and developed, while hope seen as an *emotion* may be interpreted as something that happens to us and is beyond our control (Eliott, 2005). Along with all the different conceptualizations of hope, cognitive and emotional, subjective and objective, involuntary and voluntary, comes the "possibility of non-congruence between different aspects" of hope (2005, p. 10). Thinking about hope in some inclusive and consistent manner was not becoming easier; it was becoming harder. But when hope became a variable to be measured and "correlated with just about anything," the possibilities for studying hope in different populations and in different situations became infinite, according to Eliott (2005, p. 22).

Hope Compared To Optimism

Positive psychology, in its emphasis on positive experiences,
may have overlooked the paradox that love [and hope] is more
likely to be found in the midst of suffering and pain.
— *Paul T.P. Wong*

As noted in chapter 1, optimism is defined as a positive explanatory style in which an individual believes that future events will have a favorable outcome. Seligman's (1990) research demonstrates that optimism is a valuable trait that is of great benefit to those who possess it. Similar to hope, it functions to sustain and enhance life. According to Seligman, "What we want is not blind optimism but flexible optimism—optimism with its eyes open" (1990, p. 292). "Tough-minded" optimism sees "the evils to be remedied, the injustices to be dealt with, the catastrophes to be averted" while still believing in the future (Gardner, 1990, p. 11). The leader has no choice but to be an optimist, someone who unfailingly believes in the future. The minute a leader ceases to believe in the future, he or she is no longer a leader. It was probably a leader who said, "I'd be a pessimist but it would never work out," according to Gardner (p.11).

Hope, in contrast to optimism, goes several steps step further than a positive interpretation of events. "Hope is more than distancing oneself from and delimiting the impact of failures; hope is the essential process of linking oneself to potential success" (italics original, Snyder, 1994, p. 18). Hope imagines, searches, actively waits in anticipation, and, most importantly, produces behavior directly related to what is hoped for.

> In contrast to optimism, hope is that particular approach to life which *confronts the ambiguities of human existence*. Optimism lives out an attitude of 'more of the same' usually informed by the law of human progress or evolutionary development. The logic of hope, therefore, is not one of inference but rather the logic of imagination (Italics mine, Lane, 1996 p. 60).

Hope looks squarely at what is, or is not, and imagines what should or could be, and searches for ways to bring it about. "Hope is definitely not the same as optimism. It is not the conviction that something will turn out well, but the certainty that something makes sense, regardless of how it turns out," according to Vaclav Havel (1993, p. 68). Conviction gives hope its strength, not probability.

> It's the action, not the fruit of the action, that's important. You have to do the right thing. It may not be in your power, not be in your time, that there'll be any fruit. But that doesn't mean you stop doing the right thing. You never know what results come from your action. But if you do nothing, there will be no result (Gandhi, 2006).

It would be a mistake, however, to equate hope *only* with visible action. Erick Fromm (1968) described hope as having a paradoxical nature that is simultaneously active and passive. While hope is not passive waiting, neither is it the "unrealistic forcing of circumstances that cannot occur" (p.9); rather, it is a state of ever readiness, both consciously and unconsciously, for the not yet, characterized by "an inner readiness, that of intense but not-yet-spent activeness" (p.12).

Snyder's Hope Theory

Hope Theory is a well-established cognitive model that views hope as the communication between our expectations and our desires, involving goals, agency thinking, and pathways thinking (Snyder, Cheavens & Michael, 2005). Rather than viewing hope as an emotion (Farran, Herth, & Popovich, 1995), Hope Theory assumes that hope cognitions causally drive emotions. Or as Block (2005) states, "change your thinking, change your life" (p. 1).

Snyder and colleagues have developed several measurements of hope: children's hope scale, trait hope scale, and state hope scale (Snyder, McDermott, Cook, Rapoff, 1997). These yardsticks are designed to indicate whether an individual possesses low hope or high hope in relation to goal attainment. Extensive research has demonstrated the reliability of these scales; state hope scale in indicating high or low hope possessed by an individual at a specific point in time, and trait hope scale in whether an individual possesses the characteristic of hopeful thinking in general. While state hope, not surprisingly, is less stable, trait hope, once developed within an individual, is stable over time (Snyder et al., 1997). Although Snyder's hope scale "has been criticized for its narrowness, its emphasis on success and goal attainment, for its

34

lack of focus on the emotional side of hope" (Hope News, 2006, p. 2), it has clearly demonstrated the importance of hope in accomplishing anything.

Goals

The "cognitive anchor" of hopeful thinking is the goal (Snyder, Cheavens & Michael, 2005, p.105). Goals fall into two general categories, 1) positive approach goals, or 2) negative avoidance goals. Goals have future *pull* (as opposed to push). They are the *not yet* that we desire, even when framed in negative terms, such as a desire to avoid something painful. Goals are reviewed in greater length in the section on hope and leadership.

Waypower

Waypower (pathways thinking) involves accessing our personal resources, our skills and knowledge, which may include the decision to learn new skills, in order to imagine a way to reach the goal. The person with high hope is capable of imagining a credible way to reach the goal along with alternative routes to be used if necessary. In this iterative process, the high hope person can reflect upon and evaluate their progress and make adjustments as necessary (Snyder et al., 2005). The mental flexibility to imagine alternative pathways is an especially useful coping mechanism as we inevitably encounter difficulties and challenges in the process of pursuing our goals.

Willpower

Willpower (agency thinking) is the motivational component of hope and involves our perception of our ability to effectively use those routes we have identified in order to reach the goal. Willpower or agency becomes especially significant when goals become blocked. Agency thinking is related to Self-efficacy Theory, in which Bandura (1977) stated, "an efficacy expectation is the conviction that one can successfully execute the behavior required to produce the outcome" (p. 193). Self-efficacy should not be defined as a personality trait, but rather as an individual's belief in their ability to coordinate skills and abilities to achieve goals in particular situations (Maddux, 2002). An individual may believe a particular course of action will lead to the accomplishment of the goal, but doubt their ability to complete that course of action. Individuals high in willpower or self-efficacy are less likely to give up when reaching goals becomes harder.

"Hope has a significant positive correlation with self-esteem," according to Snyder (1999, p. 211). Self-esteem consists of a person's sense of meaning and significance, and, like self-efficacy, is also related to motivation. As a result of their research on motivation, Ryan and Deci (2004) developed Self-Determination Theory (SDT), which describes 3 fundamental psychological needs for high self-esteem. The needs are (a) relatedness, (b) competence, and (c) autonomy. Organizations with leaders that are able to create environments that fulfill all three needs are likely to have committed and intrinsically motivated employees. SDT and Hope Theory will be revisited in the sections on nonprofit organizations and hope and leadership, as theses two theories suggest ways a leader might build an environment that fosters intrinsic motivation and thereby increases hope.

Hope and Health Care

In addition to the many quantitative studies of hope, one of the earliest qualitative studies was interested in describing hope's complexity, not measuring it, and came from the field of nursing by Karin Dufault and Benita Martocchio (1985). They defined hope as "a *multidimensional* dynamic life force characterized by a *confident* yet *uncertain* expectation of achieving a *future* good which, to the hoping person, is *realistically* possible and *personally significant*" (italics original, 1985, p. 380). This definition of hope incorporated many elements of previous definitions while remaining flexible enough to allow for different notions of hope, according to Eliot (2005). Hope could be viewed as an emotion or a cognition, as derived internally or externally, and, importantly, the person who hopes is the one to conclude whether their hope is realistic or not.

Moreover, Dufault and Martocchio proposed two spheres of hope, generalized and particularized, according to Eliot (2005). Generalized hope is not tied to any particular concrete or abstract object, while particularized hope is tied to a particular outcome, good, or state of being. Further, hope has six dimensions (a) affective, (b) cognitive, (c) behavioral, (d) affiliative, (e) temporal, and (f) contextual. Eliot (2005) argued, "Respectively these dimensions draw upon notions of hope as emotion, cognition, agentic, communal, transformative, and meaningful" (p.23). She acknowledged that this as an "oversimplification" and "that these derived categories are neither mutually exclusive nor exhaustive" (p.23). However, hope conceptualized in this way is inclusive of notions of hope as emotion or cognition, as located in reality or not. In short, this eclectic of hope could be freed from being an either/or phenomenon.

The predominant research on hope is focused on the hope of the individual and not on a socially constructed view of hope. Several studies attempt to place hope within community and present hope as a "discourse" that encapsulates cultural meanings, and which fulfills a variety of functions (Good, Good, Schaffer & Lind as cited by Eliot, 2005, p. 25). In a review of Averill, Catlin, & Koo Chon's book *Rules of Hope,* Eliot (2005) found an interesting tension in which they construed hope as an emotion, yet having a strong cognitive element—involving goal directed behavior. A significant consequence of the social constructionist conceptualization of hope is the acknowledgment that hope might be constituted differently by different cultures. Eliot (2005) concluded:

37

What was new in these social constructionists deliberations over hope was the emphasis placed upon the functional significance of hope, particularly on the social level…hope was construed as more than just as an individual variable, but as a social variable, shaped by the mores and values operative within the society, culture, or subculture under examination. At the same time, hope was perceived as producing effects beyond the level of individual well-being. (p. 27)

Section Summary

An explosion of interest in the subject of hope has produced a wealth of studies in the social sciences that contribute to our understanding of hope from multiple perspectives, in different circumstances, and even come with suggestions of how hope can be developed or manipulated through intention and deliberate action (Cheavens, Michael & Snyder, 2005; Farran, Herth, & Popovich, 1995; Snyder, 2000b). For more information on the history of hope research and how hope is conceptualized from a variety of perspectives, see *Interdisciplinary Perspectives on Hope* (Eliot, 2005). In addition, *The Hope Foundation of Alberta* has been assembling resources for scholars interested in learning more about hope since 1992 (The Hope Foundation of Alberta, 2006).

In spite of all the research on hope, there is still no consensus on a definition of hope. As the research on hope multiplies and as we attempt to reconcile the different aspects of hope which come into conflict, researchers will not only be concerned with what hope is, but what we *do* with it. The purpose of this study involves what leaders do with hope. The next section looks at leadership in the social sector.

Nonprofit Organizations and Leadership

This study looks at how hope functions in the leadership of 2 chief executive officers and 1 executive director of social service nonprofit organizations. First, this section consists of a brief review of how nonprofit organizations differ from business and government organizations. Second, the role of a nonprofit leader is described and contrasted with role of leaders in the business and government sectors. Third, Bolman and Deal's (2003) four-frame model of all organizations is reviewed, including the findings of an analysis of the leadership of nonprofit executive directors based on the four frame model.

Nonprofits Compared to Other Organizations

Business organizations provide goods or services in exchange for payment and government organizations control and regulate on behalf of taxpayers. On the other hand, 501(c)(3) nonprofits exist for the benefit of the public. Nonprofits are donor funded and inherently value-driven. Their values are implicit in their mission. The product is a changed human being, according to Drucker (1990), and that makes nonprofit organizations fundamentally human-change agents, regardless of whether their mission is to promote the arts or feed the homeless.

This fundamental difference in the purpose of nonprofit organizations has implications for how hope functions in nonprofit leadership. Hope is always related to something we care about. Our hope reflects our values. Nonprofit organizations are sometimes described as "values expressive" as they are instruments of collective action related to serving the public good (Jeavons, 2005, p. 205). Executive directors and employees of nonprofits often have the opportunity to act on their values to a greater extent than they would in the private sector. A compelling mission is a nonprofit organization's greatest strength in attracting and keeping employees (Drucker, 1990). The motivation of employees to work toward the achievement of an attractive mission often overshadows low pay, long hours and few material perks, according to Elbert (2005).

Motivation

Research shows motivation is a critical component of both hope and leadership (Snyder, 2000; Porter, Bigley & Steers, 2003). In research on the nature of motivation, Self-Determination Theory (SDT) (Ryan & Deci as cited by Porter, Bigley & Steers, 2003) distinguishes intrinsic from extrinsic motivation. Extrinsic motivation is the performance of an activity in order to receive some tangible reward whereas intrinsic motivation is the performance of an activity for the satisfaction of the activity itself. In comparison studies between people who are intrinsically motivated and people who are extrinsically motivated, the intrinsically motivated people exhibit more interest, excitement and confidence in the performance of their work. Ryan and Deci concluded individuals must pursue personally meaningful goals that fulfill basic psychological needs in order to experience optimal well-being. In other words, people must be engaged in activities that they find meaningful to be intrinsically motivated. Research shows that 61% of employees of nonprofit organizations were primarily motivated by the "chance to make a difference" compared with 32% of governmental workers and 20% of employees in the private sector (Light as cited in Elbert, 2005).

There is a temptation, especially on the part of business leaders, to assume nonprofits need to operate more like a business. Jim Collins, leadership scholar and author of *Good to Great* (2001), argued most businesses are not great: They are mediocre. Why would we want to import mediocrity to the nonprofit sector? Collins (2005) argued that business thinking is not the answer; "We must reject the idea—well-intentioned, but dead wrong—that the primary path to greatness in the social sectors is to become more like a business." In response to the oft-repeated notion by business leaders that the social sector is in desperate need of discipline, Collins (2005) responded,

> Most businesses also have a desperate need for greater discipline—disciplined people who engage in disciplined thought and who take disciplined action—that we find in truly great companies. A culture of discipline is not a principle of business; it is a principle of greatness.

Collins suggested that the type of leadership required in the social sector to become great might be the model of leadership that businesses adopt in the future. Nonprofit leaders must appeal to intrinsic motives, while business leaders often rely on high salaries, comprehensive benefits, and numerous perquisites to attract the "best" talent. Nonprofit leaders must be careful in the hiring process as they cannot fire people as easily as business leaders. Nonprofit leaders can rarely compete with the private sector in terms of employee pay and must attract and rely on the unpaid resource of volunteers. A nonprofit leader who is able to attract and orchestrate the efforts of intrinsically motivated and self-disciplined people, people who share organization's values and a vision, has a much better chance of building a great organization than the business leader who relies primarily on the power of extrinsic motivators. Drucker (as cited in Gardiner, 2006) recognized that nonprofit organizations were poised to become models for organizational transformation when he observed:

> In two areas, strategy and effectiveness of the board, they are practicing what most American businesses only preach. And in the most crucial area – the motivation and productivity of workers – they are truly pioneers, working out policies and practices that business will have to learn tomorrow… The nonprofits…are forging new bonds of community to active citizenship, to social responsibilities, to values. (p. 66)

Extrinsic motivators like high salary, paid leave, stock options and retirement benefits *do* motivate people (Porter, Bigley & Steers, 2003.)

Although as powerful a motivator as financial compensation and extrinsic motivators are, they are not as powerful as a person's unique intrinsic motivation.

> In Calcutta, the nun Mother Teresa, who one day could no longer endure seeing, on her way to school, deathly ill and dying people lying in the street without receiving any humane aid, persuaded the city government to let her have an empty neglected building which she turned into the famous Hospital for the Dying. A reporter, observing her work with the poorest of the poor, commented to her that he would not do 'anything like that' if he were paid a thousand dollars a day for it, she is said to have replied, tersely and magnificently, 'Neither would I.' (Pieper, 1997, p. 236)

According to Self Determination Theory (SDT), "people are most alive, motivated and vital when they satisfy basic psychological needs" (Ryan and Deci, 2004, p. 474). SDT identified 3 *intrinsic* needs that all people must fulfill in order to grow: (a) relatedness, (b) competence, and (c) autonomy. To create an optimum environment, a leader must foster community, make sure people have adequate training, are in positions suitable to their strengths, and are allowed to be self-directed as much as possible. When needs for relatedness, competence and autonomy are met, people experience high self-esteem, which is highly correlated with hope (Snyder, 2000a). Ryan and Deci maintained, "acceptance without autonomy represents alienation" and "relatedness without competence represents amotivation and helplessness" (p. 476).

Intrinsic motivation (willpower) is a key component of hope (Snyder, 1994). Leaders who understand the power of intrinsic motivation can enhance both hope and motivation by: (a) establishing an open, supportive and trusting environment where people feel free to talk about their values, (b) ensuring that people are placed in positions, or allowed to craft positions, that match their skills and strengths, and (c) ensuring that people are respected as free and autonomous, as well as responsible and accountable. All three needs must be met for high intrinsic motivation (Ryan & Deci, 2004).

The nonprofit sector may be in a better position to address the essential elements of motivation—relatedness, competence, and autonomy—than the business sector, in which the emphasis is clearly focused on transactional leadership involving extrinsic motivators. John Jacob Gardiner (2006) suggested "nonprofit organizations are winning the hearts of workers and thus offering insight regarding the nature of the change required to transform shared governance in all organizations: *well-defined missions, functioning/empathic boards, trained volunteers, and values centered communities of learners*" (italics original, p. 66).

Role of the Nonprofit CEO or Executive Director

Nonprofit organizations differ from the private sector in the nature of the relationship between the chief executive office (CEO or executive director (ED) and the board of directors. The CEO or ED must maintain relationships with multiple constituencies but none is more critical than his or her relationship with the board of directors (Drucker, 1990; Herman, 2005). The board of directors and the leader of nonprofit organizations must forge a uniquely close relationship in order to accomplish the mission. In business, most boards show little interest until there is a crisis (Drucker, 1990). In contrast, the nonprofit board is deeply committed to the organization's mission, often leads the fundraising, oversees and collaborates with the executive director, and is legally responsible for the achievement of the mission. Meddling would be a more common problem for nonprofit boards than a lack of involvement. According to Drucker (1990), a strong board that provides the right kind of leadership is usually indicative of the hard work of a CEO or ED who has shaped that board and serves as its conscience.

Effective nonprofit leaders accept the fact that they fill a psychologically central role in their organizations (Herman & Heimovics, 2005). While it has long been recognized that leadership is an activity not limited to a position or a role, and that a conceptualization of leaders as heroic is dangerous (Heifetz & Linsky, 2002; Lipman-Blumen, 2005), research has shown that the most effective executive directors accept responsibility for enabling their boards to carry out their leadership roles (Herman and Heimovics, 2005).

> Our research shows that chief executives, board members, and others regard the chief executive as primarily responsible for the conduct of organizational affairs. This is, we think, a fact of life in nonprofit organizations, however strongly we or others might want it to be otherwise. (p. 168)

The centrality of the leadership role, along with a conviction regarding the moral imperative of the mission, may make nonprofit leaders particularly susceptible to a heroic conception of leadership. Becker (1973) claimed that the basic motivation of all human behavior is to deny the terror of death. Jean Lipman-Blumen, in *The Allure of Toxic Leaders* (2005), argued that our desire for achievement, or to engage in heroic projects, is driven by fear of death. It is an attempt to secure our own immortality through what Otto Rank referred to as our "immortality projects," or the efforts that will cause us to live on in the minds of others (2005, p. 59). Achievement through pursuits that are culturally recognized as worthy, like the role of a nonprofit leader, shore up our self-esteem and the need to be seen as significant individuals in a meaningful world. Lipman-Blumen (2005) argued "culture promotes the lie that we can transcend death by great acts of achievement, with *leadership* serving as the prime vehicle" (italics mine, p. 117.) The danger of a heroic conceptualization of leadership may be especially great in nonprofit organizations as "they are prone to consider everything they do to be righteous and moral and to serve a cause" (Drucker, 1990, p.11). Radical self-reflection and openness to the feedback of others is necessary for leaders to maintain a grounded perspective. Humor also

44

helps. "All you earnest young men [and women] out to save the world—please, have a laugh," urged Reinhold Niebuhr (Quoteworld, 2006).

The nonprofit leader must be diligent to serve the organization's mission in an appropriate and trustworthy manner. Trust, according to Jeavons (2005), is the lifeblood of nonprofit organizations. Dependence on voluntary donors for funding makes maintaining public trust more critical for nonprofits than business or government. Any breach of ethics can have a dramatic effect on funding and the ability to pursue the mission. In addition to being above suspicion ethically, nonprofits must prove that they are exercising good stewardship or risk losing donors to other organizations where it is believed donations will be used more effectively. Furthermore, a nonprofit leader's power and influence are typically not derived from social position or wealth. The social capital that a nonprofit and its executive director have is a direct reflection of perceived trustworthiness (Jeavons, 2005).

An Organizational Model

According to the four-frame model of organizations developed by Bolman and Deal (2003), *all* organizations function as a system or factory (the structural frame), behave like a family (the human resource frame), are arenas or jungles (the political frame), and represent a temple or theatre (the symbolic frame). Life in an organization is complicated, ambiguous and unpredictable. Using multiple perspectives reduces the chances of leaders misreading a situation and increases the likelihood of developing more effective strategies for action, argued Bolman and Deal (2003). The purpose of the four-frame model is to provide a way for leaders to *reframe* any situation within their organization from four distinct perspectives.

The self-reflective executive director will recognize the value assumptions that underlie each frame in order to be aware of her own preferences and limitations in her ability to view her organization holistically. According to Bolman & Deal (2003), the structural frame values clear goals and objectives and the development of rational procedures to achieve organizational effectiveness. The human resource frame values people, their hopes and aspirations, and seeks to maximize opportunities for personal growth and development. The political frame recognizes there are always competing needs and trade-offs and it "assumes ongoing conflict or tension over the allocation of scare resources," (Herman & Hemovics, 2005, p. 165). The political frame sees building coalitions and developing personal and organizational power as necessary for effectiveness. The symbolic frame views organizations as socially constructed communities that are knit together by the development of shared meaning and the power of vision. Hope in the performance of leadership should function differently within each of these frames.

Herman and Heimovics (2005) examined executive leadership of nonprofits using the four-frame model and found some interesting distinctions in the predominant frames used by effective executives versus comparison executives. Analysis showed the structural frame was the dominant frame used by effective executives and comparison executives, but the comparison executives were "almost twice as likely to employ the structural frame and 70 percent more likely to use the human resource frame than the political frame" (2005, p. 165). The effective executives used the political frame significantly more than their counterparts.

> By contrast the political frame was the second most dominant
> frame for the effective executives, who were almost as likely to
> use it as the structural frame. Most significant, effective
> executives were twice as likely as the comparison executives to
> engage in actions defined by the political frame. (2005, p. 165)

In addition to discovering that effective nonprofit executives relied upon the political frame much more than comparison executives, their research uncovered an interesting extension regarding the political orientation of effective executives. Namely, the executives disavowed their political orientation: "whereas the use of the political frame was the most strongly distinguishing and most important criterion of executive effectiveness, executives without respect to effectiveness acted in political ways and advocated a less politicized philosophy," according to Herman and Heimovics (2005, p. 165).

What accounted for the unacknowledged use of political skills by effective executive directors? Herman and Heimovics conducted a second study using Argyris's (1993) distinctions between espoused theories and theories-in-use as a coding criterion. Their findings indicated the incongruity was related to a difference in the executive's espoused theories (expressed beliefs) and their theories-in-use (actual behavior). The executives were often unaware of the discrepancy between the values they espoused as their leadership philosophy and how they actually behaved. Even though effective executives were twice as likely as comparison executives to exhibit political skills and behavior, both sets of executives espoused a leadership philosophy reflected by the structural and human resource frame.

Both the structural frame, with its emphasis on rationality, and the human resource frame, with its emphasis on people, favorably aligns with popular conceptions of leadership and hope. The use of political skills may be perceived as socially unattractive. The strong use of the political frame is especially intriguing, according to Herman and Heimovics (2005), as it subordinates order and rationality (the structural frame) and concern for others (the human resource frame) in favor of marshaling power, developing coalitions, bargaining, negotiating and jockeying for position among stakeholders (Bolman and Deal,

47

2003). However, the use of the political frame, by nonprofit leaders especially, may be more complicated than the conclusion that it subordinates rationality and concern for others. The relationship between the political frame and hope is explored in chapter's four and five, where it is suggested a primary motivation for using the political frame by nonprofit leaders is based on a pragmatic and rational concern for others.

Section Summary

There are 3 obvious distinctions between public service nonprofit organizations and corporate and government organizations. First, nonprofits exist to serve a mission, while the purpose of business (in general) is make a profit and government to control and regulate. Second, for serving a mission that is deemed of benefit to the public these organizations receive tax deferred status. Third, they are primarily funded by donations and/or grants.

Nonprofit organizations function similarly to business and government organizations in that all organizations function from four distinct perspectives or frames: structural, human resource, political, and symbolic (Bolman and Deal, 2003).

What is distinctive about public service nonprofit leadership is that it is founded upon a moral imperative (Herman, 2005). The fact that nonprofits are value-driven necessarily makes them politically-driven. Advocacy on behalf on the organization's mission is unavoidable if executive directors are to be effective. Yet it may not be acceptable for the nonprofit leader to espouse a political agenda even while she must exercise political skills.

Finally, research indicates that effective executive directors of nonprofits do four things well: (a) accept and act on their psychological centrality, (b) provide board-centered leadership, (c) emphasize leadership beyond their organizations' boundaries, and (e) think and act in political ways, according to Herman and Heimovics (2005).

Hope and Leadership

"Leadership is one of the most observed and least understood phenomena on earth," according to Burns (1978). There are more than forty leadership theories described in *The Encyclopedia of Leadership* (Burns, Goethals & Sorenson, 2004). Extensive research has produced many different categories of leadership theories: great-man, trait, situational, psychoanalytic, humanistic, contingency, transactional, and transformational (Bass, 1990). Categories of leadership are popular as they simplify and help us conceptualize leadership in ways that allow us to talk about it. However, simplification of leadership can result in "overgeneralization and faulty inferences," cautioned Bass (1990), who predicted that as leadership research evolves, simple theories of leadership will "give way to more sophisticated conceptualizations" (p. 36).

The purpose of this section is not to provide a review of the many different conceptualizations of leadership, but rather to suggest some ways in which leadership concepts are related to hope within the context of this study. Research on leadership is viewed through the lens of the two theoretical underpinnings of this study described in chapter 1: (a) existential themes, and (b) Snyder's Hope Theory. The first section is a review of some the ways in which the existential themes of authenticity, freedom, accountability, anxiety, and meaninglessness are related to hope and leadership. Leadership concepts that emphasize community, engagement, pluralism, freedom, accountability, self-transcendence and the cultivation of meaning will be shown to foster hope. Also, characteristics of effective and ethical leadership, like trustworthiness, are critical to the cultivation of hope. Second, examples show how the components of Hope Theory (goals + willpower + waypower) are related to research on leadership. Finally, examples are suggested for how hope might function in the performance of leadership.

Philosophical Framework

As stated in chapter 1 under theoretical framework, the broad philosophical underpinning of this study is derived from the existential themes of anxiety, suffering, despair, death, authenticity, freedom, accountability—and faith, hope and love. Faith, hope and love are not themes that commonly come to mind when we think of existentialism and some of the more famous existential thinkers. Nietzsche declared, "God is dead" and Sartre said, "Hell is other people." Existential philosophers are sharply divided in their response to the question: Why do we exist? Some conclude life is absurd, without purpose, so you are free to choose your own purpose. Others, through faith, reach a very different conclusion (Buber, 1970; Frankl, 1984; Kierkegaard, 1980; Tillich, 2000; Marcel, 1962). Faith, hope and love *become* themes of many existential philosophers after confronting anxiety, suffering, death and the burden and guilt that accompanies freedom of choice.

Furthermore, it is occasions of anxiety, suffering, despair and death that most clarify love and meaning, hope and leadership (Frankl, 1984). An existential perspective views the nature of persons as more than biologically determined organisms. "Unless the individual is free to constitute the world in any number of ways, the concept of responsibility has no meaning," insisted Yalom (Yalom as cited in Snyder, Higgins, & Stucky, 1983, p. 13). To put it bluntly, people possess both the freedom and the responsibility to choose how they respond to every circumstance in life, even if they don't chose the circumstance (Block, 1993). But it is often easier to believe that we have no choice, as "choice is a two-edged sword" (Snyder, et al, 1983, p. 14). This section on hope and leadership emphasizes the relationship between hope and the awareness of our freedom and responsibility.

Leadership is inherently philosophical. "There is no neutral ground from which to construct notions and theories of leadership," according to Heifetz (1994, p. 14), "because leadership terms, loaded with emotional content, carry with them implicit norms and values." It is not surprising then that a plethora of theories, perspectives, definitions, and metaphors exist which attempt to describe and explain leadership in a coherent fashion. To date, no single perspective on leadership clearly reigns in the field of leadership studies (Harter, 2006). Rather than searching for the one best theory, definition, or metaphor, it makes more sense to try to integrate all valid perspectives on leadership. When we encounter divergences in leadership theories, instead of wondering which "theory, definition, or model is correct...we should *expect* divergences and integrate them as best we can," according to Harter (italics original, 2005, p. 78).

Leadership as Relationship

Burns (1978) noted a serious failure in the study of leadership has been "the bifurcation between the literature on leadership and the literature on followership. The first approach often sees the leader as either a saint or demon. The second approach is based on "the conviction that in the long run, at least, leaders act as agents of their followers" (1979).

> The leadership approach tends often unconsciously to be elitist; it projects heroic figures against the shadowy background of drab, powerless masses. The followership approach tends to be populistic or anti-elitist in ideology: it perceives the masses, even in democratic societies, as linked with small, overlapping circles of conservative politicians, military officers, hierocrats, and businessmen. (p. 3)

Too much emphasis on one approach over the other can be blinding, cautioned Burns. He argued that leadership is a "structure of action that engages persons" and that "the processes of leadership must be seen as part of the dynamics of conflict and power" that are linked to collective purpose (1978, p. 3). The only way to avoid the "conceptual straitjacket" (p. 31) of thinking of leadership too narrowly is to understand that first and foremost it is a relationship, a relationship with a purpose, a relationship with multiple constituencies and multiple degrees of engagement. Leadership and power are not things; they are *relationships* (Burns, 1978). Hope is also a relationship (Marcel, 1951/96).

Leadership and Conflict

Furthermore, the potential for conflict [as well as the potential for hope or despair] permeates human relations, and "that potential is a force for health and growth as well as for destruction and barbarism" (Burns, 1978, p. 37). Leadership itself is grounded in conflict as conflict unites as well as divides. Conflict, according to Burns, "galvanizes, prods, motivates people" and "leadership acts as an inciting and triggering force in the conversion of conflicting demands, values, and the goal into significant behavior" (p. 39). In much the same way hope itself is grounded in despair. The process of overcoming despair also galvanizes, prods, and motivates us to take action based upon our values and goals. Burns (1978) argued, "leaders, whatever their professions of harmony, do not shun conflict; they confront it, exploit it, and ultimately embody it" (p. 39).

Likewise, despair is confronted in order to ultimately become hope (Marcel, 1951/1996). The first step in actively overcoming despair is a clear-eyed acknowledgement of the situation followed by the acceptance of our freedom, our choice, even if that freedom is severely limited by our particular circumstances (Groopman, 2004). Freedom should not be confused with entitlement (which is actually a denial of freedom and responsibility). Freedom is always accompanied by *responsibility* and *anxiety* over conflicting choices (Koestenbaum & Block, 2001).

Thanks to Freud, most people are well aware of the defense mechanisms of denial, displacement, repression, scapegoating and projection when these traits are manifested in the negative behavior of *other* people. But the majority of people remain unaware of the extent to which our institutions and our relationship with those in authority are a reflection of our own "escape from freedom" (Fromm, 1965; Block, 1993). In a Faustian bargain, followers give leaders power in exchange for the illusion of security and protection from the hard choices in life (Block, 1993). In truth, no leader, whether saint or barbarian, can assume our existential freedom and accountability (Fromm, 1965).

Responsibility, Meaning and Hope

Leaders and followers need to forge a new social contract in which both share responsibility for the results of the contract (Heifetz, 1994). "The paradox is that we have created a world so dependent on the centrality of leadership that citizens and employees have developed a learned dependency," contended Block (1998, p. 90). Block reported that when people are asked what they want, they most often respond: better leaders. They want kinder, wiser, more competent leaders who shelter and protect them and always act in their best interest. "People seek the safety and comfort of someone at the top keeping the vision alive, promising a safe and prosperous tomorrow. They keep asking management to define their roles, develop a better pay system, judge their performance more objectively," according to Block (p.90). The passive belief that the solution to our problems is better leadership is both a myth and an excuse. Block argued,

Avoiding responsibility, compliance, and caution on the part of employees and citizens is a bigger problem than control and self-centeredness on the part of leaders. The solution is not to create better leaders, it is to explore how to become accountable citizens. (p. 90)

We create our lives through our choices and it is the recognition of our freedom and responsibility that allows us to create meaning (Block, 1998). Each moment presents an opportunity and "what matters is not the meaning of life in general but rather the specific meaning of a person's life at a given moment" according to Frankl (1984, p. 113), and the *choice* that moment affords. Meaning comes from the awareness that each day is contingent—death is certain—along with the recognition we can choose to love and be loved. "Love gives meaning to what you do, whether in a corporation, a community, a classroom, or a family," according to Heifetz & Linsky (2002, p. 210). When we accept our freedom and accountability, we can choose to create caring, compassionate, community within organizations (Block, 1998).

Leadership as Activity

Most definitions of leadership involve the use of influence, but leadership is more than influence. Further, leadership is often coupled with power and associated with a person who occupies the top position in a hierarchy. Heifetz suggests we stop focusing on leadership as a position or set of characteristics, and instead "focus on leadership as an activity—the activity of a citizen from any walk of life mobilizing people to do something" (1994, p. 20).

Moreover, the adaptive leadership model offers a significant paradigm shift from the typical perspective on influence. Heifetz asked, "Imagine the differences in behavior when people operate with the idea that leadership means influencing the community to follow the leader's vision versus leadership means influencing the community to face its problems?" (1994, p.14). He positioned leadership as an adaptive activity "the central task of which is getting people to clarify their values and to recognize that there are competing needs and trade offs" (p. 22). Conflict of over competing values and motivations exists even within a community of people who are in complete agreement with the organization's mission, insisted Burns (1978).

> Conflicts over priorities are seated in, and probably exacerbated by, a pluralism of *personal* needs and motivations that may seem irrelevant to the public goals of the department but in fact enlarge the triangle of commitments, loyalties, and purposes. (italics mine, p. 377)

An adaptive approach to leadership implicitly recognizes competing value perspectives by allowing people to grapple with finding solutions to problems that *require* the clarification and prioritization of values (Heifetz, 1994). Leaders who respect autonomy and pluralism foster freedom and accountability. Leaders who try to protect their followers from harsh realities and difficult choices foster "learned helplessness" (Seligman, 1990).

The Role Of Followers

Leadership research is increasingly focused on the role followers play in the leadership dynamic (Burns, Goethals & Sorenson, 2004). Research has shown that the unconscious desires and behaviors of followers can foster toxic behavior in leaders (Heifetz, 1994; Kellerman, 2004; & Lipman-Blumen, 2005). Likewise, followers who abdicate personal responsibility or fail to oppose unethical leadership invite leaders to run amok (Gardner, 1987; Koestenbaum & Block, 2001). As research on the role of followers accumulates, along with education and technological advances, there is evidence followers are becoming more intentional in crafting their relationship with leaders (Burns et al, 2004). Even now, research suggests the typical hierarchy of leadership in America no longer exists (Kouzes & Posner, 2002). A look back at the patriarchal

55

relationship between doctor and patient a generation ago compared with the doctor and patient relationship today is a good example of how old hierarchies are flattening. Information that once was the possession of the privileged is now only a click away thanks to technology (Kouzes & Posner, 2002).

Honesty, Trust and Hope

> *I have a higher standard of principle than George Washington.*
> *He cannot lie; I can, but I won't.*
> *—Mark Twain*

The number one attribute of admired leaders is honesty (Kouzes & Posner, 2001). According to Roset (2004), the ability of leaders to influence hope is directly related to their perceived credibility and trustworthiness. "We know that trust is the foundation of any good relationship—and fundamental to getting extraordinary things done," stated Kouzes and Posner (2002, p. xxii). Trust is defined as the "firm reliance on the integrity, ability, or character of a person or thing" and is related to "reliance on something in the future; hope," and means "to believe: *I trust what you say*," (italics original, Soukhanov, 1992). In this study "trust" and "believe" are used synonymously, as believe is defined as "to expect, suppose or think" and "have faith, confidence, or trust" (1992). Trust and hope are joined at the hip; it is impossible for one to move forward without the other as hope always implies belief in someone or some thing (Pieper, 1997.)

> *There is no worse mistake in public leadership*
> *than to hold out false hopes soon to be swept away.*
> *—Winston Churchill*

Honesty is essential for the development of trust; trust is essential for the development of hope (Pieper, 1969). People in leadership positions, like doctors, often have access to information we do not have and often assume that they know what is best for us, according to Groopman, (2004). Regardless of the motive, whether to protect us, achieve compliance, or avoid the discomfort of confronting difficult choices, withholding vital information that we need in order to develop real hope is an insult to human dignity (2004). It reflects a lack of faith or trust in the other person, and is often based on an elitist assumption that the other person cannot handle the truth. Leaders who lie, mislead, or withhold important information rob us of the capacity to develop realistic hope and make informed choices. "Clear eyed hope gives us the courage to confront our circumstances and the capacity to surmount them…true hope has no room for delusion," insisted Groopman (2004, p. 210).

Trust and Servant Leadership

The importance of trustworthiness in leadership is emphasized in some leadership models more than others. It has been over three decades since Robert K. Greenleaf introduced the concept of servant leadership. Spears claimed, "the times are only now beginning to catch up with Greenleaf's visionary call to servant-leadership" (Spears, 1998, p. 1). According to Greenleaf (1998), the best test of servant leadership is summed up in this question: "Do those served grow as persons; do they, while being served, become healthier, wiser, freer, and more autonomous, more likely themselves to become servants?" (p. 43). As he grew older, Greenleaf raised the standard of servant leadership higher by adding to his test of servant leadership this question: "What is the effect on the least privileged in society; will he or she benefit, or, at least not be further deprived?" (p. 43). Finally, Greenleaf raised the bar still higher by insisting the servant leader should act in such a way that "no one will willingly be hurt by his or her action, directly or indirectly" (p. 43). In attending to the needs of others, Frankl (1984) asserted, it is the one who serves who benefits most.

The more one forgets himself—by giving himself to a cause to serve or another person to love—the more human he is and more he actualizes himself. What is called self-actualization is not an attainable aim at all, for the simple reason that the more one would strive for it, the more he would miss it. In other words, self-actualization is possible only as a side-effect of self-transcendence. (p. 115)

Service to others in the pursuit of a collective vision inspires trust. Too often leaders are seen as "self-symbols," not as "servants of the dream," consequently, there is not enough trust in the institution by any of its constituencies for meaningful achievement (Greenleaf, 1998, p. 87).

Trust and Social Justice

> *Example is not the main thing in*
> *influencing others. It is the only thing.*
> —*Albert Schweitzer*

Although the *language* of service has been widely adopted, the experience of service is hard to find (Block, 1996). The notions of service and stewardship may reflect our intentions for leading our organizations but they do not reflect the reality. According to Block (1996) leaders have done little to change the distribution of power, purpose and reward, which remain concentrated at the top. Block argued, leaders support organizational structures and behave in ways that are a "testimony to self-interest" (1996, p. xxi). "Hope for genuine organizational reform resides in reshaping the politics of our work lives, namely how we each define purpose, hold power, and balance wealth," according to Block (1996, p. 5). Justice calls for leaders who are willing to level the playing field.

Some think the idea originated with ice cream maker Ben & Jerry's (Lager, 1994), but it was Plato who thought basic fairness dictated that no one person in the community earn more than five times the pay of the average worker.

Drucker warned in the 1980's that the growing pay gap could threaten the very credibility of leadership (Drucker as cited in *BusinessWeek*, 2002).

> No leader should earn more than 20 times the company's lowest-paid employee. His reasoning: If the CEO took too large a share of the rewards, it would make a mockery of the contributions of all the other employees in a successful organization. (2002)

Drucker's standard seems quaint today. One of many egregious compensation packages of 2006 is the $1.6 *billion* dollar option package offered to William McGuire of UnitedHealth Group while "more than 40 million Americans lack health insurance" according to a report from Knowledge@Wharton (2006). The report also mentions a retirement package of $400 million given to former Exxon CEO Lee Raymond, in 2006, as consumers face soaring gasoline prices. A Wharton school accounting professor sees nothing wrong with Raymond's retirement package as long as it disclosed.

> Disclosure is key, he stresses, using Lee Raymond's Exxon retirement package as an example. That type of package is *fine* as long as [boards and executives] contract up front, as long as it's disclosed to stakeholders and as long as the stakeholders have a right to question the pay structure. (italics mine, Knowledge@Wharton, 2006)

Gross inequity that has become institutionalized, like the inordinate pay gap between those in leadership positions and workers, fosters distrust that leads to disillusionment, disengagement and hopelessness (Block, 1993). The most profound impact of the inequities that are being institutionalized today will be experienced by the young (Snyder, McDermott, Cook & Rapoff, 1997), those yet to be hardened by cynicism, who still dare to dream big dreams—dreams on which the future of the planet depends, dreams that will be thwarted by institutionalized obstacles and oppression which turn the concept of equal opportunity into a joke.

To boast is always a cry of despair,
except in the young it is a cry of hope.
—Bernard Berenson

"The relationship between hope and justice has simply not been studied," according to Jevne (2005, p. 3). But we know intuitively that social justice has a profound impact on how, or if, we experience trust and hope. Roberto Peña's reflections on his childhood experience of racial prejudice while attending a predominately white school illustrate the chilling effect of injustice upon budding hope (2005). Memories, the present, and the perceived possibilities of the future influence hope. "Memories of injustices are often seared into our memories and the depth of the scar inflicted is a function of the degree and duration of the injustice" (Jevne, 2005, p. 3). In the laboratory of a school classroom, Jevne observed, "inequities that demoralize, that assault hope," were built into the educational system (Jevne, 1994, p.9). As a teacher, she noted, "How easy it is to become an assailant. Noting the inequities and my own insensitivity was the beginning of my search for new ways of being" (p. 9).

Leaders can easily become hope assassins through insensitivity, a lack of self-reflection, and the toleration of inequities. If they want to be trusted, leaders must be willing to challenge unjust policies and practices that may benefit them personally. According to Heifetz (1994), "no one gets to the top without representing the interests of the dominant factors in the system" (p. 238). It takes courage and conscience effort to challenge "the routine ways in which people throughout the system collude in maintaining the status quo" (p. 238). Recognizing and eliminating racism, sexism, ageism, classism, cronyism and any other -ism that privileges some at the expense of others shifts the focus to a higher plane, off individual concerns to collective concerns. Unless inequity and injustice are addressed there is no collective vision.

Leaders must be willing to reject concepts based upon "competition, market rivalries and their seductions, in favor of concepts like integration, inclusiveness, inter-and intra-dependence, environment, equity, ecology, transcendence, love and finally race as place," according to Peña (2005, p. 23). The former paradigm maintains a climate of distrust; the later paradigm builds a climate of trust.

> "Once injustices are voiced, hope can begin its work" and from "the consciousness of injustice, hope movements are born," according to Jevne (2005, p. 3). It [hope] functions as a bridge between poverty and plenty; anger and resolution; war and peace; prejudice and tolerance; between what is and what could be. It asks not only for a righting of the situation but for a healing of the heart, for a *reclaiming of the expectation of goodness in the future.* (italics mine, 2005, p. 3)

The leadership of organizations in the nonprofit sector may be in a better position to foster a climate of trust than the business sector for several reasons. First, they are likely to be more acutely tuned to social justice issues, including those in the workplace. Second, the values-driven nature of nonprofit organizations and the high reliance on volunteers calls for leaders who are inclusive and appeal to the intrinsic motivation of their fellow workers. An open and inclusive leadership style is more congruent, than, for example, a transactional leadership style, for a mission-driven organization that seeks to attract dedicated employees and volunteers. Open and inclusive leadership is often associated more with women than men.

According to Dym and Hutson (2005), "The majority of people working in nonprofits, both as employees and volunteers, are women" (p. 6). Researchers are divided when it comes to differences in leadership styles between women and men, some see women's leadership as distinct (Lipman-Blumen, 1996), and others do not (Dym & Hutson, 2005).

61

Researchers argue that when placed in the same circumstances, men and women operate in similar ways. When large organizations have prescribed certain modes of behavior, women who rise will have mastered those behaviors. In fact, women who rose in male-dominated organizations…behaved in ways associated with men: hierarchical, competitive, and the like. (p.7)

However, the women who started their own companies or rose in women-dominated organizations were less hierarchical, more democratic, more collaborative, and tended to nurture younger employees—all characteristics that contribute to a climate of trust and hope.

Second, nonprofit organizations are *expected* to be mission driven. Business organizations, in market economies, are under high pressure to attract investors and meet shareholder's expectations of growth, and therefore companies are often tempted to treat profitability as their raison d'être. They must make a profit to be sure. Companies "need profits in the same way as any living being needs oxygen. It is necessary to stay alive, but it is not the purpose of life" (De Geus as cited in Bolman & Deal, 2003, p. 395).

New Metaphors for Leadership

Leadership that allows people to thrive, not merely survive, requires new ways of thinking about leadership. Replacing the heroic myth of leadership, and the patriarchal paradigm in which it is packaged, requires new metaphors, new ways of conceptualizing leadership, according to John Jacob Gardiner (2006).

A new metaphor, transcendent leadership, answers a planetary call for a governance process which is more inclusive, more trusting, more sharing of information (its happening anyway via the internet), more meaningfully involving *associates* or *constituents* (almost anything but "followers"), more collective decision making through dialogue and group consent processes, more nurturance and celebration of creative and divergent thinking and a willingness to serve the will of the collective consciousness as determined by the group – in essence, a leadership of service above self. (italics original, p. 72)

Conceptualizing leadership as a relationship (Burns, 1978), as service (Greenleaf, 1998), as stewardship (Block, 1993), and as transcendent (Gardiner, 2006), accompanied by the steadfast refusal by leaders to be seduced into the limiting role of hero or patriarch, will move us in the direction of freedom and accountability within our organizations (Koestenbaum & Block, 2001).

Snyder's Hope Theory and Leadership

In research that began nearly two decades ago C.R. Snyder began to formulate Hope Theory. An early definition of hope was, *"hope is the sum of the mental willpower and waypower that you have for your goals"* (italics original, Snyder, 1994, p. 5). A later definition expanded to become *"hope is the sum of perceived capabilities to produce routes to desired goals, along with the perceived motivation to use those routes* (italics original, Snyder, 2000a, p. 8). With the help of numerous contributors and a great deal of research, Snyder and colleagues (Snyder, Cheavens and Michael, 2005) offered the following definition of hope: "Hope is a positive motivational state that is based upon an interactively derived sense of successful (a) agency (goal-directed energy), and (b) pathways (planning to meet goals)" (p. 105). Hope Theory resonates with research on effective leadership. If the three fundamental elements necessary for high hope in individuals consist of goals, willpower and waypower, wouldn't these fundamental elements for developing hope be applicable in organizations as well?

> *Where there is no vision, the people perish*
> *—Proverbs 29:18*

No credible theory of leadership fails to acknowledge the importance and power of creating goals (Burns, 1978). In the context of organizational leadership, the terms vision, purpose, and goal are sometimes used interchangeably although these terms are distinct. A goal is an aim or specific target. Vision is the ability to think about the future with imagination and wisdom. It represents an aspiration or dream of what the future could be. Vision becomes a sense of purpose when we commit ourselves to goals that reflect and support the realization of the vision.

According to Heifetz (1994), "leadership requires, perhaps first and foremost, a sense of purpose—the capacity to find the values that make risk-taking meaningful" (p. 274). Purpose is fueled by our values, our intrinsic motivation. "A *sense* of purpose is not the same thing as a *clearly defined* purpose," Heifetz argued (italics mine, p. 274). A sense of purpose is more like a global positioning system (GPS) that continually informs and guides us in our choices and the selection of goals. In the context of organizational leadership, high hope involves creating a vision that is shaped by group values, translated into specific goals and strategies (pathways) to reach those goals, along with belief in the organization's ability to execute those strategies effectively.

Goals

We cannot think, feel, will, or act
without the perception of a goal.
—Alfred Adler

"All leadership is goal-oriented," insisted Burns (1978, p. 455). Samuel Coleridge (1912) claimed, "Hope without an object cannot live" (p. 447). John W. Gardner (1990) asserted, "leadership is a subtopic" of a larger topic, namely "the accomplishment of group purpose" (p. xvi). Goals are emphasized in virtually all leadership theories (Barnard 1938/1968; Burns, 1978; Bass, 1990; Gardner, 1968; Greenleaf, 1998; Heifetz, 1994; Kouzes and Posner, 2002). Although the *importance* of goals is commonly understood, how goals function in relation to hope is not commonly understood.

Warning Signs: Anger and Apathy

Organizational leaders have the responsibility of ensuring that the goals that are set can be met. Research has shown that feelings of anger and hostility are indications that people feel blocked in their ability to reach their goals (Snyder, 1994). Regardless the impediment, whether it is other people, organizational policy, environment, a lack of resources or skill, limited pathways thinking, low self-efficacy—whatever the reason—people become hostile when they cannot get what they want (1994). In the journey toward hopelessness, it is easier for a leader to intervene at signs of anger and frustration than it is at signs of despair and apathy.

> In psychological death, one is left in a relatively enduring state of mental apathy toward life goals…The demise of hope usually involves the move from hopeful thinking, to rage and despair at the blockage of goals, to the ending point of apathy about goals in general. (1994, p. 116)

As was mentioned in chapter 1 under the heading theoretical framework, willpower (motivation) does not necessarily correspond to waypower (pathways or agency thinking). Goals must be accompanied by both motivation and agency to equal high hope. "The anger of high-willpower/low waypower people, for example, arises from their inability to get around the impediments in their lives," according to Snyder (1994, p. 116). Generally, when people become blocked in the pursuit of important goals the result is frustration and anger. This can be good news for the leader in the same way that physical pain is good for alerting us to a problem that needs medical attention. Hostility is easier to recognize than despair, and, although few people relish the idea of confronting hostility, it is easier to address than apathy. Anger has energy. Conflict and struggle are signs of engagement. In apathy, the struggle itself has been abandoned.

According to Snyder (1994), "much of the rage we see in society reflects the first stage of the demise of hope" (p. 118). If goal blockages are strong, such as in the case of institutionalized oppression related to prejudice or poverty, and the blockages continue in spite of a person's willpower and waypower thinking, the person blocked may begin to feel impotent, and "the rage may give way to despair and cynicism" (p. 118). Cynicism is a mask for deeper feelings of disappointment, frustration, anger and despair. Leaders would be wise to pay attention to expressions of anger and cynicism.

Burnout and Goals

Research has linked the phenomenon of burnout with blocked goals (Snyder, 1994), but the concept of burnout is often attributed to stress and overwork. "One of the insidious characteristics of burnout is that once people have succumbed, they tend to explain their negative feelings in terms of external events or circumstances" according to Snyder, McDermott, Cook, & Rapoff (1997, p. 113). Attempts to remedy burnout usually focus on external factors that do not identify and address the underlying issues. Hence, a solution to burnout is not as simple as scheduling a vacation.

The opposite of burnout is sometimes described as "flow," which occurs when a person is attending to and is mentally "invested in realistic goals, and when skills match the opportunities for action" (Csikszentmihalyi, 1990, p. 6). More psychological than physical, research has shown that burnout has more to do with the perception of our failure to reach our potential in relation to the achievement of meaningful goals than with being overworked.

> One of the primary researchers on the topic of burnout, Ayala
> Pines, has suggested that burnout can be understood as an
> instance in which one's important work-related goals are
> frustrated by blocking circumstances. For example, the goal of
> most teachers is to convey information and stimulate thinking,
> but the large class sizes and need to attend constantly to

discipline may block this goal. Therefore, it is not just stress, but also the goal blockages that actually cause burnout. (Pines cited in Snyder, 1994, p. 142)

Nurses should be especially vulnerable to burnout reasoned Snyder (1997), as increasing administrative responsibilities, coupled with a limited staff, restricts their ability to spend time with and comfort each patient, perhaps thwarting the reason they became a nurse in the first place. "Researchers studied the mindsets of nurses to test the proposition that burnout could be understood as a manifestation of the loss of hope," according to Snyder (1997), and reached the following conclusion.

Those nurses who experienced the least hope, as measured by Snyder's Hope Scale, also had the highest emotional exhaustion and depersonalization and the lowest sense of accomplishment on the Maslach Burnout Inventory. Furthermore, results revealed that, the *lack of a sense of accomplishment especially predicted low hope*. Burning out, the researchers concluded, reflects our repeated perception that we have been unable to reach important goals. Burnout is the extinguishing of hope. (italics mine, p. 142)

Note that the individuals most susceptible to the phenomenon of burnout are individuals who have been filled with hope at some point. Snyder (1994) observed wryly, "one cannot burnout…without previously having been on fire" (p.141).

Autonomy and Hope

Motivation is correlated with individual autonomy and the pursuit of personally meaningful goals. According to Ryan and Deci's (2004) Self Determination Theory (SDT), "people are most alive, motivated and vital when they satisfy basic psychological needs" (p. 474). SDT identifies three needs that all people must fulfill in order to grow: (a) relatedness, (b) competence, and (c) autonomy. When needs for relatedness, competence and autonomy are met, people experience high self-esteem, which is strongly correlated with hope

(Snyder, 2000a). For more on the relationship between SDT and leadership, see the section on executive directors and nonprofit leadership in this chapter, which specifically addresses autonomy and intrinsic motivation.

Leadership Processes and Hope Processes

In *The Encyclopedia of Leadership* (Burns, Goethals & Sorenson, 2004), leadership is described as a reciprocal interaction between leaders and followers in relation to goals.

> The effectiveness of a leader depends largely on the leader's ability to create an environment where goals are well articulated and shared, where people know the routes to be used in pursuing those goals, and where people have the requisite motivation to see goals through to fruition. (Snyder & Shorey as cited in Burns et al., 2004, p. 674)

"Leaders play a crucial role in that they help chart the directions of the groups of people who form societies," and "thus, they help to produce the agenda for the future" (Snyder & Shorey as cited in Burns, et. al., 2004, p. 675). They also suggested that people who become leaders likely do so because of their ability to inspire hope in others. Kouzes and Posner conceptualized leadership based upon what leaders *do*, and have identified several leadership processes (as cited in Burns et al., 2004). According to Snyder and Shorey, (2004, p. 674) five leadership processes correspond to the components of Hope Theory. These five processes and how they correspond to Hope Theory are shown in Table 1.

Table 1

Leadership Processes Compared with Hope Theory Processes

Posner & Kouzes Processes	Hope Theory Processes

1. Challenging the process
   a. Searching for opportunities
   b. Experimenting & taking risks
	1. Choosing challenging goals

2. Inspiring a shared vision
   a. Envisioning the future
   b. Enlisting the support of others
	2. Setting shared group goals

3. Enabling others to act
   a. Fostering collaboration
   b. Strengthening others
	3. Instilling a sense of agency

4. Modeling the way
   a. Setting examples
   b. Planning small wins
	4. Instilling pathways thinking

5. Encouraging the heart
   a. Recognizing contributions
   b. Celebrating accomplishments
	5. Taking pleasure in successes so as
	to reward continued hopeful thinking

Adapted from Hope, Snyder & Shorey, Burns, Editor,
The encyclopedia of leadership, 2004, p. 674.

Suggested Functions of Hope in Leadership

This study seeks to understand how hope actually functions in the performance of leadership. It is important to clarify that *function* represents the underlying *purpose* or *intent* of the leader in the use of hope. How hope might function is comparable to the way in which a gift might function. The function of a gift may be many different things regardless of the gift. For example, the function of a gift might be to celebrate, gain respect, express affection, show gratitude, make a point, receive something in return, create an obligation, or a number of other things. The real function of a gift is not always apparent just as the underlying purpose, the intention of the leader, is not always apparent in certain leadership behaviors.

Hope can function both constructively and destructively. Refusing to acknowledge that hope can and does function destructively in the performance of leadership is a form of denial we cannot afford. Hope should not be idealized any more than leadership should be idealized. We turn leaders into idols when we insist that they be heroic figures who must protect and save us from the harsh realities of life. To ensure hope functions constructively in the performance of leadership, leaders and followers must become aware of how hope is functioning in leadership.

Reclaiming Hope

The word hope is ubiquitous in everyday speech. It is easy to forget that our deepest hope lives closest to despair. Tillich (2000) claimed the word "hope" had lost its meaning, that it had become too common, and therefore he choose the word "courage" as a substitute for the word hope in his classic treatise, *The Courage To Be*. Indeed, *the hope to be* is not nearly as compelling. Tillich claimed, "Courage is the affirmation of one's essential nature, one's inner aim or entelechy, but it is an affirmation which has in itself the character of 'in spite of' (p. 4). Hope is intimately connected to our deepest longings, our possibility, and can function as the courage to be—*in spite of.*

Gardner (1990) saw how hope could function to elevate the lives of individuals by cultivating a sense of meaning and purpose, while at the same time focusing attention on some of society's most pressing problems. An explosion of research from the field of nursing has demonstrated hope serves a healing function (Dufault, & Martocchio, 1985; Farran, Herth, & Popovich, 1995; Parse, 1999; Eliot, 2005;). Research in biology and medicine has confirmed the healing power of hope (Cousins, 1989; Groopman, 2004). Hope fuels imagination and draws upon memory in order to solve problems (Lynch, 1965). Hope most assuredly functions in the achievement goals (Burns, 1978), in the development of self-efficacy (Bandura, 1977) and in motivation (Ryan & Deci, 2004).

Pieper (1997) argued, "the only answer that corresponds to man's existential situation is hope" (p. 98). Hope is indistinguishable from courage, according to Tillich (2000), who asserted, "Courage gives consolation, patience, and experience and becomes indistinguishable from faith and hope (p. 8). Furthermore, courage and joy coincide. "Joy is the emotional expression of the courageous Yes to one's own true being" (p. 14). Hope can function to help us participate in the self-affirmation of being-itself. Through hope we recognize our essential being, our freedom and accountability, our possibility, which provides us with "the opportunity to choose to be noble," according to Koestebaum & Block (2001, p. 245), even in ignoble circumstances.

The Dark Side of Hope

Hope deceives more than cunning.
—Vauvenargues

Even the Bible warns of leaders who use hope in order to mislead. "Watch out for false prophets. They come to you in sheep's clothing, but inwardly they are ferocious wolves," according to the gospel of Matthew (NIV, Mt. 7:15). Marx called religion the "opium of the masses" because he believed religious leaders used the hope of an afterlife to create passive compliance in the here and now (Marx as cited in Pieper, 1969). Nietzsche saw how hope could easily be manipulated, how it could be built upon a desire for domination or revenge (Atichison, 1996). Gardner (1981) claimed, "The truly modern dictator achieved his goals through people, not in spite of them. He rides their aspirations to power. He manipulates their hopes and fears (p. 56).

While not all misuses of hope have malevolent motives, even the well-intended misuse of hope has destructive consequences. One area that easily illustrates the misuse of hope is in the field of medicine. Jerome Groopman (2004), an MD, hematology and oncology specialist, respected medical researcher and professor at Harvard Medical School, with 30 years of experience in working with AIDS and cancer patients, claimed once a physician has lied to a patient, even if he told the lie with good intentions, any hope the physician would subsequently raise, no matter how truthful, would not be trusted. Although leaders in organizations typically do not deal with life and death situations in the same way that physicians sometimes do, leaders can learn a great deal from physicians in regard to the use and misuse of hope. When leaders distort the truth, withhold important information, deliberately mislead or encourage false hope, they ultimately destroy trust and foster cynicism. To encourage false hope is an injustice, according to Groopman (2004).

True hope, then, is not initiated and sustained by completely erasing obstacles. An equilibrium needs to be established, integrating the genuine threats and dangers that exist into the proposed strategies to subsume them. So when a person tells me he believes ignorance is necessary for bliss, I acknowledge that, yes, an unbridled sense of fear can shatter a fragile sense of hope. But I assert that he needs to know a minimum amount of information about his diagnosis and the course of his problem; otherwise, his hope is false, and false hope is an unsubstantial foundation upon which to stand and weather the vicissitudes of difficult circumstances. (p. 210)

Ironically, leaders who would keep hope alive through misguided notions of protection are often the most likely to undermine it. Leaders who wish to be ethical and effective must be first become aware of how they use hope in the performance of leadership, and then they must become intentional in the constructive use of hope, an essential requirement of which is a commitment to be scrupulously truthful.

Section Summary

This section of the literature review related hope to leadership through the lens of the 2 theoretical underpinnings of this study: (a) existential themes, and (b) Snyder's Hope Theory (2000a). Ways in which the existential themes of authenticity, freedom, accountability, and meaningfulness intersect with the research on hope and leadership were suggested. The character trait of trustworthiness in a leader was emphasized as critical for the development of a climate of hope within an organization. Additionally, the relationship of social justice to the development of trust and hope was noted. Leadership concepts that emphasize community, engagement, pluralism, freedom, accountability, self-transcendence and the cultivation of meaning were shown to foster hope.

Several of the ways in which Snyder's Hope Theory (2000a) are related to research on effective leadership were described. The importance of the role

73

that goals play in fostering hope was stressed and the dynamic nature of how goals function in relation to agency and motivation was emphasized. Finally, examples of how hope might function both constructively and destructively in the performance of leadership were suggested.

CHAPTER THREE

RESEARCH DESIGN AND METHOD

The purpose of this study was to develop a better understanding of how hope functions in the performance of leadership by leaders of nonprofit organizations. This chapter describes the research design, methods used to conduct this study, assumptions of the researcher, and limitations of the research.

Design

A phenomenological design was selected in order to develop a deep understanding of the dynamic, contextual and relational nature of hope and leadership as experienced by the participants. This approach was selected for two reasons. First, the majority of the literature on leadership is prescriptive, telling us more about how to lead and much less about how leaders actually lead, according to Dym and Hutson (2005). They argued that description should come before prescription. A phenomenological study focuses on description. Second, hope and leadership are abstract concepts that are experienced in the human mind and therefore do not lend themselves to quantitative methods such as statistical measurement and prediction (Harter, 2006). A phenomenological study seeks understanding versus prediction, textured analysis versus counting, and meaning versus statistical relationships (Smith, 2005).

Data

The primary data consisted of observation and in-depth interviews of 3 leaders of nonprofit organizations. Public service nonprofits (as opposed to member-benefits) were chosen for this study because the nature of the challenges they face can make it difficult for them to maintain hope. They must continually solicit money and resources and are often under funded in relation to the demand for services. They deal with people in need on a daily basis, people who may be facing life-threatening situations. Additionally, the services they provide are often controversial and politically charged. Since nonprofits are inherently values-expressive, it follows that if they were unable to succeed in their mission they would be tempted to lose hope.

While leadership is now widely understood as an activity in which anyone may engage, 2 chief executive officers and 1 executive director were chosen for this study as the position they occupy within the organization carries an expectation of leadership (Barnard, 1968; Herman & Heimovics, 2005).

Observation and interviews were conducted while "shadowing" each leader for a period of 3-4 days. Shadowing in the context of this study refers to the researcher accompanying the participants in their daily activities at work in order to gain experience or insight. This method of data collection allows the researcher to become intensely involved with the participants in their work environment and to ask questions in a natural context that facilitates an on-going dialogue. Walking along side of the participants as they went about their work increased the opportunity for a deep understanding of the phenomenon under study as experienced by the participants (Stacks and Hocking, 1999).

Participation in the research was restricted to 3 leaders for several reasons. First, additional time was needed to allow the participants to consider concepts related to the research that required self-reflection on their part, noting, "self-reflection does not come naturally," (Heifetz and Linsky, 2002, p. 51). Second, the subject matter was sensitive and participation in the study required a significant time commitment. Hope was examined in relation to despair. The literature indicates despair is experienced in some sort of encounter with one's limitations, according to Goldsmith (1987). I anticipated difficulty in securing participants due to the deeply personal nature of study and the time commitment that would be required. Two of the participants I knew personally. The third

76

participant was a personal referral by one of the other participants. Participants who already know and trust the researcher, or trust the person who refers the researcher, are the most likely to agree to participate in a study that involves exploring the experience of hope and despair (1987).

Third, in a phenomenological study the number of participants is not as important as the qualifications and ability of the participants to adequately address the research question (Murphy, 1980). Participants who are knowledgeable in relation to the research are considered to be what many qualitative researchers call "key informants," according to Murphy (1980). Care was taken to select participants who were key informants.

Finally, a restricted sample size forces the researcher to go deep as opposed to shallow. A large number of participants would produce a large amount of data, all of which would require handling by the researcher. According to Foss and Waters (2007), time spent collecting and analyzing a large amount of data from a broad number of participants often results in a more superficial analysis than if the researcher spent the same time collecting and analyzing data from a smaller sample size.

Document analysis augmented the data gathered from the taped conversations and observations. One participant provided a personal journal for review and another the records of a daily Internet blog dating back several years. Additionally, a wealth of written data were available from each organization's website, annual reports, correspondence, newsletters, and public records.

Data Collection

Data collection consisted of observation, in-depth interviews and analysis of written documents. The primary method of data collection consisted of shadowing the participants for a period to 3-4 days each as they went about their work. An in-depth interview was conducted while shadowing the participants. The interviews were taped with a small recorder in a variety of settings: while driving in a car, walking down the street, eating lunch, stopping for a cup of coffee, waiting in a lobby, riding an elevator, or while in sitting in an office. Conducting the interviews in this manner provided a natural context in which to ask questions and was conducive to developing an on-going dialogue. According to Stacks and Hocking (1999) in-depth interviews should be used when seeking to understand the participants' personal interpretation of social interaction or events that inherently contain a value or policy orientation.

The participants were selected from well-established nonprofit organizations that have been providing services for a minimum of 10 years and whose annual operating budget is no less than 5 and no greater than 10 million dollars per year.

Participants who were knowledgeable in relation to the research, "key informants" (Murphy, 1980), were selected for this study. The criteria for selection of participants was (a) a minimum of 5 years in the position of executive director or chief executive officer, (b) 50 years of age or older, and (c) an expressed interest in effective leadership coupled with the willingness to participate in an interview process that would be time consuming and which might elicit feelings of discomfort. Participants allowed the researcher to shadow them for 3-4 days each in the performance of their duties. Taped interviews were transcribed at the end of the shadowing period. Field notes were immediately recorded after each contact with the participant(s).

Prior to contacting the participants, a pilot study was performed with 3 individuals known to the researcher. One was a former executive director of a public service nonprofit organization, another was a graduate student at Seattle University, and the third was a faculty member of Seattle University's Nonprofit Leadership Program. The purpose of the pilot study was to test the interview protocol in order to develop and refine the questions prior to engaging the participants selected for the study.

Data Analysis

The data from the taped interviews were transcribed and analyzed according to the primary elements of the grounded theory method (Glaser & Strauss, 1967). The constant comparative method was first developed by Glaser and Strauss and later elaborated upon by Lincoln and Guba (1985). This theory draws from the assumptions of a phenomenological approach to the analysis of data. The method of data analysis emphasizes the use of qualitative rather than quantitative data and is typically used by researchers who gather data through interviews, the examination of written documents and observations (Grove, 1988). The method is based upon an inductive, rather than a deductive, process of investigation of data. The grounded theory, or constant comparative research method attempts to stay tied to the data and let the data suggest the themes of the study. This method is designed to generate a theory from the data, rather than verify an existing theory. According to Glaser and Strauss (1967),

> "a pivotal belief…of most social scientists is that through the
> processes of verification and quantification, social phenomena
> can be reduced to those 'primary qualities' of an 'absolute and
> objective' reality. Glaser and Strauss contend that this can be
> accomplished only through avoiding one of the most potentially
> confounding variables: the immediate context of the everyday
> world of people." (Glaser and Strauss as cited by Lewis, 1992,
> p. 286)

The researcher was engaged in a process of constant comparison while simultaneously collecting and analyzing the data in order to refine, categorize and integrate the data into a coherent theory (Taylor and Bogdan, 1984).

Grounded theory, or constant comparative method, was chosen as a method of data analysis because, while the research on both hope and leadership

79

are growing, there is a lack of research specifically in the area of how hope *functions* in the performance of leadership as experienced by the leader. Two major benefits of grounded theory according to Glaser and Strauss (1967) are: (a) its ability to fit the situation that was actually researched and (b) its recognizability and usability by those involved in similar situations as the study because its basis is familiar data (Radich 1986). Lincoln and Guba (1985) added a procedural variation to the constant comparative method referred to as *member checking*. At the member checking stage the researcher offers her reconstruction of the data to the participants in the study and they determine whether the reconstruction is a reasonable representation of reality (Grove, 1988). The participants in this study were asked to review the data and researcher's analysis.

Methodological Assumptions

"There is no 'theory-free' study of anything, no 'pure description'…that is not already enabled by a point of view or set of assumptions" according to Martin Jaffee (2002, p. 2). No qualitative researcher is a *tabula rasa*, or someone who can step outside of herself in order to analyze a phenomenon from a neutral position. I do not presume to be objective nor do I believe the findings of this study constitute definitive knowledge; rather, they provide a description, an approximation, and a provisional one at that (Damasio, 1994).

While I do not presume objectivity, I am aware of my own perspective and how it has been shaped. I strive to be open to new ways of experiencing the world, new interpretations and paradigms. The principle of openness is central to phenomenological approaches to research where the researcher becomes closely involved with the phenomenon under study, according to Dahlberg and Halling (2001). Research on a human experience is not defined by formal steps or protocol, but rather is characterized by a striving for openness that allows the

80

phenomenon and it's meaning to reveal itself. This openness requires that the researcher "endure periods of experiencing chaos," and to "resist demands for absolute certainty and order" (Dahlberg and Halling, 2001, p. 20). The most open and reflective phenomenological researcher, however, is a participant in her own research, complicit in the construction of the knowledge derived from the data.

Researcher's Bias

I have experienced the loss of hope in achieving organizational goals. I have witnessed colleagues lose hope. I know firsthand how devastating the effects of a collective loss of hope within an organization can be; it robs people of life and immobilizes the organization. In Gardner's classic treatise, *On Leadership* (1990), he does not single out hope as a distinct subject. But I believe the need for hope is the implicit subject on every page. Gardner expressed deep concern at the pervasive immobilization exhibited by so many people in the face of so many serious problems.

> I do not find the problems themselves as frightening as the
> questions they raise concerning our capacity to gather our forces
> and act. No doubt many of the grave problems that beset us have
> discoverable, though difficult, solutions. But to mobilize the
> required resources and to bear what sacrifices are necessary calls
> for a capacity to focus our energies, a capacity for sustained
> commitment. Suppose that we can no longer summon our forces
> for such effort. Suppose that we have lost the capacity to
> motivate ourselves for arduous exertions in behalf of the group.
> A discussion of leadership cannot avoid such questions. (p. xvi)

Gardner focused on what he called the "issues behind the issues" in leadership, which he identified as motivation, values, social cohesion and renewal (1990, p. xvii). Research on hope in other disciplines has demonstrated that these issues are closely related to our capacity to develop hope (Eliot, 2005).

Historical research provides descriptions of a multitude of leaders who were effective in the use of hope—in spectacularly destructive ways. Hitler was undeniably effective at exploiting the hopes of a majority of Germans in order to influence them to follow him. Hope can, and does, function destructively in the performance of leadership. Those who accept leadership positions must also accept responsibility for fostering either cynicism or hope. We do not need leaders who are good at coercion, seduction, or secrecy. We need leaders who help us recognize our freedom—the possibility and the responsibility (Koestenbaum & Block, 2001). Only real hope will galvanize us to face difficult problems, to accept responsibility to act in the present, rather than to retreat into some form of escapism or to become apathetic and cynical. I believe we need real hope and leaders who can help us develop it.

CHAPTER FOUR

PRESENTATION AND ANALYSIS OF DATA

The purpose of this study was to develop a better understanding of how hope functions in the performance of leadership by 3 leaders of public service nonprofit organizations. The findings drawn from the data are unique to the 3 participants and do not represent leaders in general. First, this chapter includes a brief review of the data collection process. The story of the discovery process experienced by the researcher is interwoven with the presentation of data in order to make the data more accessible. Second, similarities between the participants are noted. Third, the participants are introduced. Fourth, the findings are presented according to 8 dominant themes: (a) personal values, (b) education, (c) justice and social justice, (d) fear, faith, and courage, (e) authenticity, (f) mission, (g) social capital, and (h) leadership. Finally, a conceptual schema is suggested for how these themes contribute to the hope of these leaders and how hope functions the performance of their leadership.

The participants' stories reflected a commitment to truth, purpose, freedom and responsibility—a striving for authenticity. Data revealed that love was a primary motivation for these leaders. The personal values of the participants led to choices that have resulted in the development of authentic leadership in the service of a social purpose. This study suggests that for these leaders hope is kept alive through caring relationships and primarily functions as the virtue of courage within community.

The Data Collection Experience

Two chief executive officers (CEO's) and one executive director (ED) were shadowed, for a period of 3-4 days each, while they carried out their

83

professional responsibilities. An in-depth interview was conducted over the course of shadowing the participants. Shadowing refers to accompanying each participant as they went about their daily activities at work. The interviews were taped with a small recorder in a variety of settings such as while driving in a car, walking down the street, eating lunch, stopping for a cup of coffee, waiting in a lobby, riding an elevator, and while in sitting in an office. Conducting the interviews in this manner provided a natural context in which to ask questions and was conducive to developing an on-going dialogue.

I discovered while collecting the data that pursuing an abstract concept like hope by asking pre-determined questions from a list was not nearly as fruitful as watching, listening, and becoming engaged with the participants as they went about their work, asking questions only when appropriate. "By contrast, data collected according to a preplanned routine are more likely to force the analyst into irrelevant directions and harmful pitfalls," claimed Glaser and Strauss (1967, p. 48). I taped a telephone conversation I had with my husband the evening after the first day of data collection.

> Tim, you're not going to believe this. This is so exciting! I am
> beside myself! I don't know whether to laugh or cry. My whole
> study is upside down. It's on its head. [Tim: "Well, is that a good
> thing?] It's a GREAT thing! It's what you want in
> education—the discovery process—you want your assumptions
> challenged. But on the other hand, it's like…Oh my goodness!
> (laughs) My interview protocol is irrelevant—it's flat out *not*
> relevant. (laughs) It's not that my questions are bad. They just
> aren't relevant.

Direct questions proved the least effective. I was reminded of Frankl (1984), who did not consider hope itself a goal, but saw it as a by-product of a meaningful life. When I came at hope directly it eluded me; it was best approached obliquely. I realized that even though I was conducting a phenomenological study, I had approached collecting the data with a quantitative mindset. I gave up trying to control the interview in order to make sure we plumbed my pre-determined questions in favor a more authentic encounter with the participants. Research on a human experience is not defined by formal steps or protocol, but rather is characterized by a striving for openness that allows the phenomenon and its meaning to reveal itself, according to Dahlberg and Halling (2001). The nature and meaning of a phenomenological study finally clicked; what had previously been theoretical became real for me.

In addition to the data gathered from the taped conversations and observations, a wealth of written data were available from each organization's website, annual reports, correspondence, newsletters, and public records. One participant allowed me to read her journal in which she described and reflected upon her life from her childhood to the present day. Deeply personal, it provided an understanding of what has shaped her in a way that would have been impossible to discern without it. Another participant's daily Internet blog, with entries dating back several years, was an invaluable source of data.

Similarities Among Participants

The type and size of the public service nonprofit organization, the age of the participants, and their years of experience serving in a leadership capacity are similar. The annual operating budget of the each organization is between 5-8 million dollars a year. The participants ranged in age from their late 50's to early 60's. Each has served in a leadership capacity as CEO or ED from 15-25 years, although not always within the same nonprofit organization. The participants each stated that they were unconcerned about privacy issues in regard to this research. However, their names and the names of the nonprofit organizations in which they work have been changed to pseudonyms, and the identity, location, and distinguishing features of their organizations have been disguised to ensure anonymity.

Introduction to the Participants

The participants' pseudonyms represent an archetype which corresponds to my impression of a dominant character strength unique to each of them. The first archetype is the Biblical prophet Amos. A prophet is, "a person gifted with profound moral insight and exceptional powers of expression" (Soukhanov, 1992). The prophet Amos lived during the peaceful reign of Jeroboam II (786—746 B.C.), a period where Israel attained a height of national prosperity never reached again. Amos was called "to preach harsh words in a smooth season...for grave injustice in social dealings...and shallow, meaningless piety" (1973, The New Oxford Annotated Bible, RSV, p. 1107). Amos the prophet spoke truth to power.

The second archetype is an Amazon warrior in Greek mythology, Amynomene (Ah-men-o-meme). The Amazons were a nation of strong, beautiful, women warriors. The origin of the word *Amazon* is unknown, however folk etymology explained the word as being a derivative of the preface "a," meaning "without," followed by "mazos," meaning "breast." This folk etymology is supported by the folktale that Amazons cut off one breast to facilitate archery (Ruffell, 1997). Amynomene means *Blameless Defender*.

The third archetype is Athena, who was a Greek goddess of wisdom associated with mentoring heroes as well as strategy and tactics in battle. She is often called the Goddess of the City, a nurturer of community, a the protectress of civilized life and artisan activities who is said to have sprung fully grown and in full armor from the head of Zeus (Encyclopedia Mythica, Retrieved March 28, 2007).

Coincidently, the participants' pseudonyms all begin with the letter "A". In the presentation of the data their stories are woven together, which can make distinguishing one participant from the other confusing, especially the two women. In order to make it easier to identify the participants when there is a change in perspective in the text, I have added an archetype tag to each of their pseudonyms: Amos *the Prophet*, Amynomeme *the Defender*, and Athena *the Communitarian*.

Amos the Prophet

I first met Amos nearly twenty years ago when he came to Seattle to speak to a local Christian congregation about starting a food resource center. Even then, the approach he advocated to address the needs of the poor emphasized renewal versus charity. What he recommended was innovative and inspiring, yet required more than dollars and donations. It required a broader worldview and commitment that the congregation did not possess; a more traditional charity model was adopted by the Seattle group.

I ran into Amos off and on over the next decade during Pepperdine University's Annual Bible Lectures. Our conversations were always brief, but I could sense he was moving at light speed in a different direction than organized religion's typical response to the poor: a combination of charity and judgment. He was up to something much more hopeful. Although I had not seen or spoken to him in years, he immediately came to mind when I settled on a research focus for this study and many of the examples selected to illustrate the themes found in the data are from Amos.

Amos grew up in a mid-sized town in the Northwest and was raised by good, hard-working, middle-class parents. He has a Master's degree in History, a graduate degree in Divinity and a passion for liberation theology. Something happened to him as he was learning to become a Christian minister. He fell in love with the radical Jesus: the Jesus who befriended whores, lepers, the poor and the oppressed. This turned out to be a different Jesus than the one favored by most rich, white, evangelical churches, especially in the South. His first church was located on a boundary line between a wealthy white neighborhood of grand old historic homes and a very low-income black neighborhood of ramshackle, sub-standard housing. He was ejected rather quickly from this affluent congregation for inviting the neighbors to church. Next he served at a congregation in New Orleans and got a real close look at poverty, before he became the minister for a well-to-do church in another large Southern city, one of the wealthiest cities in America.

At this new congregation, he faced what was to be a defining moment in their history together. In the 1980's they decided to participate in the Sanctuary Movement, a religious and political movement of approximately 500 congregations that helped Central American refugees, who were fleeing death squads, by sheltering them from Immigration and Naturalization Service authorities. This proved to be too much for many members who chose to leave the congregation. Those who stayed were changed by their encounter with the refugees. They became less judgmental and formed a stronger, more ecumenical community, which prepared the way for what would come next.

Amos thought the church should be more involved with the poor, especially in a city of such extreme wealth along side of abject poverty. The congregation agreed and they started a food pantry in the mid 1980's that soon became KINSHIP, a separate 501(c)(3) nonprofit organization. In 1997, after battling hunger everyday for nearly a decade, Amos and the KINSHIP leadership realized that hunger was a symptom of deeper issues associated with poverty. They began to look for ways to address the many obstacles that prevent people from escaping poverty. Today, KINSHIP has programs and services that address poverty issues related to hunger, health, housing, legal, education, and employment. The annual budget has grown from $200,000 dollars to over eight million dollars. KINSHIP shows no sign of slowing down as they continue to develop innovative programs and form collaborative partnerships. KINSHIP has the broadest reaching mission of the three organizations in the study. Amos reminds anyone who will listen that, "Poor people aren't the problem, poverty is the problem."

> Poverty crushes people. Very often people who are interested in the work we are doing will say something like, 'Why are you trying to do so many different things? Why don't you just focus on two or three main areas? What you really need is to discover your niche and work from there. You would find it easier to fund your organization if you did that!' I try to be polite and to explain: poverty can't be 'niched.' Funding is not the point, although it is a perpetual struggle. Overcoming poverty in the lives of men, women and children is the goal and the challenge for us. This is why we must attack on many fronts. Securing food for your family is great. But if you are sick with no physician or if you have a major legal problem or if you are unemployed or underemployed or if you have no reliable transportation or if you live in substandard housing, food could be the least of your problems

Amynomene the Defender

I first met Amynomene four years ago when we worked together on a social justice project. She has a doctorate in Educational Leadership and is a highly accomplished individual. I looked forward to working with her, as she is the real deal, a firebrand, as a friend of mine is fond of saying of authentic people, "there's no baloney in that sandwich" (personal communication, Roberto Peña, 2006). Yet, Amynomene and I clashed while working together. Although the project was successful and would prove to be sustainable, our relationship with each other had become tense and distrustful. Neither of us was content to let our relationship end this way so we sat down together to work it out. We had a fierce, frank, courageous discussion—it would have been much easier to simply part company as we no longer needed to work together. But, as is often the case in strong personality clashes, we discovered how we had misinterpreted the words and actions of one another.

Her culture and experiences are radically different from mine. I am a privileged, white, middle-class woman who grew up in a home and neighborhood where my safety was never threatened. She is an African American woman who experienced the kind of persistent trauma in her childhood that would have been hard for an adult to survive, let alone a defenseless child. Yet, she has turned her pain into a source of strength in her tireless and fearless defense of vulnerable children. As we took the time to understand one another we realized that, while we might approach problems differently, we share the same values. Our relationship grew into a genuine friendship.

Amynomene is a live wire. Grab her in the wrong place and you are going to get a jolt. But connect with her in the right way and you will be lit up—infused with energy. She has given me a new set of eyes and has consistently expanded my awareness of the subtle forms of racism and economic oppression that are still prolific in America.

She is the executive director (ED) of the nonprofit organization, HOME, a school for homeless children in the Pacific Northwest. HOME's mission is to educate, nurture and advocate for children whose families struggle with the risk or reality of homelessness. While the focus of activity is around educating children in Kindergarten through 6th grade, HOME has discovered that often the best way to help a child is to help the child's parent or family. While attempting to meet the educational needs of homeless children, HOME also helps parents find employment, permanent housing, and other support services, as they work to help stabilize families.

When Amynomeme was a young girl she attended a march with Dr. Martin Luther King Jr. She saw the dream and has never lost sight of it. That dream has fueled a lifetime devoted to standing up for the disenfranchised, especially vulnerable children. She is politically astute and a powerful advocate for education and equity for the poor. She literally burns rubber. In the short time I have known her she has replaced all of the tires on her car driving to and from the State Capital. She lobbies one Senator or Representative after another to oppose legislation that would negatively impact children and low-income families, or to support legislation that would benefit them. The latest evolution of her political savvy is to participate in drafting legislation.

Athena the Communitarian

Athena was the only participant with whom I had not developed a relationship prior to this research. I assumed that because my questions were deeply personal that an existing, trusting relationship would be necessary for the participants to be unguarded. Frankly, I was surprised and relieved to find Athena to be so open and forthcoming. I accompanied her to breakfast meetings, staff meetings, luncheon meetings, executive meetings, collaborative meetings, conflict resolution meetings and even dinner meetings. Nothing she did was off limits to me during our time together.

Furthermore, she has a keen interest in research on leadership. She has a Master's degree in Public Administration and is a graduate of the Harvard Business School Executive Education Program in Governing for Nonprofit Excellence. "The first and last task of a leader is to keep hope alive" is more than a slogan to her (Gardner, 1968, p. 134). John W. Gardner was a member of the Stanford University faculty at the time he died, in 2002, while Athena was attending the Stanford Leadership Studies program. She recalled, "It was a deeply moving experience to be on that campus at that time." Like Gardner, she has an unswerving commitment to equality, justice and building community.

Athena grew up an only child in a quintessential *Leave It To Beaver* small town in the Northwest. Everybody loved their neighbor, there was no poverty, and there was no discrimination, or so it seemed. A book changed her life. The book was *Angels in Hell's Kitchen,* by Tom McConnon (1959). Told from the viewpoint of a young boy, the book is full of richly developed characters and evocative images. Reading the vivid and poignant descriptions of poverty during the Great Depression in a New York City ghetto was a turning point that set Athena on a lifelong journey.

> When I went to work in 1965, it was during the Great Society and there were enormous resources available. I'd just had my 22nd birthday and I was at DSHS [Department of Social & Health Services] working with foster children and teenage mothers. I mean, I was like 2 years older than the people I was working with. I had gotten a book when I was a little girl—ten years old—my mother used to go to this clothing apparel store, and one day the owner gave me a book called 'Angels In Hell's Kitchen,' and I read that book and knew I wanted to work with people in Hell's Kitchen on the streets of New York City and I never wavered.

Athena served as ED of two nonprofit organizations, both focused on the protection, health and welfare of children and families, prior to becoming the CEO of Community Builders, whose mission is focused on building caring, confident youth and future leaders from within supportive communities. Community Builders is located in the Pacific Northwest and is the largest chapter of a national organization, Community Builders of America, that is one year shy of 100 years old. It would not be an exaggeration to describe it as the first widely organized feminist movement in America. The human liberation philosophy that is the underpinning of the organization's values has allowed it to morph with the times and embrace inclusion before the idea of inclusion became popular.

Currently, Community Builders is playing an important role in developing community groups for the large number of immigrants in the region from all over the world, many of whom speak little or no English. "Language and cultural differences are huge obstacles for immigrants," according to Athena. She is particularly proud that her organization is addressing this obstacle. As a first step, albeit a major one, Community Builders recently translated all of their extensive educational materials into Spanish.

Athena has deftly led Community Builders through a period of difficult change in order to address the needs of a changing culture. Community Builders does not have a one-size-fits-all program. They take their cue from the different communities themselves. By offering the kind of support that the community desires and needs, this organization is still as relevant today as it was nearly 100 years ago.

Presentation of Findings

The research question was how does hope function in the performance of leadership by three leaders of public service nonprofit organizations. The findings drawn from the data are unique to these three leaders and do not represent leaders in general. Eight dominant themes emerged from the data: (a) personal values, (b) education, (c) justice and social justice, (d) fear, faith and courage, (e) authenticity, (f) mission, (g) social capital, and (h) leadership. In the context of this study, the themes are inextricably related to one another and contain numerous sub-themes. Therefore, they should not be conceptualized as distinct categories, but rather as highly permeable forces working in concert.

Personal Values

You can either follow your fears or be led by your values.
—William Sloan Coffin

Values are principles or standards of behavior that represent an individual's judgment concerning what is important in life (Soukhanov, 1992). Related to values are spirituality, faith, belief or worldview—the standpoint a person adopts that explains their morality, their choices. According to Novak (1978, p. 12), "Living comes first, reflection comes afterward." Our continual interpretation of our experience constitutes a standpoint, or worldview, from which our values develop and our choices are shaped.

Values like love, courage, honesty, compassion, justice, community, gratitude and forgiveness are all evident in the participants' stories. However, if there is an underpinning belief evident in the data that has shaped the values and behavior of all three participants it is a belief in the immeasurable worth of a human being. People matter. Not only do people matter. People matter most. Time and again the data revealed that love for people was a primary intrinsic motivation for these leaders. The value they place on *life*, and especially *human* life, is paramount in their stories. Love and compassion are evident in the choices they have made to concretely engage with other human beings. According to Halling (2000, p. 143),

> To be moved, to be affected, by the situation of the other is an embodied experience, an experience of one's whole being. Thus, in 'transcending' we do not move beyond the world but deeply into it, and being affected by the 'other' we reconnect with ourselves as subjects who have some measure of freedom. In these moments, we do not turn away from the precariousness of existence but embrace all of who we are as we more fully partake of life.

94

As we move through the data according to the dominant themes, listen to what is behind the participants' stories, statements, and especially their actions. See how each participant's experience develops into a sense of purpose, how love is a necessary inference that explains many of their choices, and how their hope is sustained in relationships.

Amos the Prophet believes that people have the power, the desire, and the capacity to solve their own problems if given the chance. He likes to tell the story of when they moved their resource center into the poorest section of the city. Back then all the volunteers drove in from the suburbs and they were all white. "Relationships with the community always felt pretty much 'one down.' You know, paternalistic, neo-colonial," he said. One day he asked a volunteer, one of the leading women of the church, not to come back after he heard her lecture a homeless man who was smoking a cigarette. Additionally, Amos found that the white volunteers from the suburbs were not always dependable. They tended to show up only when it was convenient for them. KINSHIP seemed to be always short on money and resources. Then one day his world and the world of KINSHIP changed in a moment.

> I found myself facing three Hispanic mothers with their beautiful
> children. They were perfect strangers to one another and to me.
> These three delightful people were attempting to combine their
> limited English to overcome my absolute stupidity when it comes
> to speaking Spanish. We weren't getting too far. As our
> frustration grew, an older woman, Rita, walked by and I asked
> her if she could help me. I learned then, and have learned many
> times since, that this is a very important question for 'helpers' to
> learn how to ask those they seek to 'help.'

Amos and Rita were able to provide the assistance the three families sought. As the Rita was leaving, Amos thanked her profusely,

I still had not realized what an asset I had right in front of me. She had the good sense to turn back to me when she reached the door. I will never forget what she said, 'Amos, I could come back tomorrow and help you.' Rita came back "tomorrow" for nine years.

Later that same day Amos was in his office looking out the window at the "crack house" next door. He claims he received a very clear message that came in two parts.

First, I was dead wrong about the neighborhood. Even though I thought I knew what it needed, I couldn't possibly know. Second, I had been wrong to look at the community only in terms of *need*, especially material need. I should look at the neighborhood in terms of its *assets*. There are all kinds of assets besides the material variety. I thought of the woman who helped me that day. It was so clear—the truth so obvious.

Over the next forty-five days Amos set out to change the organizational culture and change it quickly. Every person who came through the door was encouraged to talk about their assets as well as their needs. They invited everyone to return and serve as a volunteer and almost overnight they had more volunteers than they knew what to do with.

People from outside the community who were our supporters questioned our sanity. 'Looks like you have the lunatics running the asylum,' one supporter said. 'These people will steal you blind,' I was told in many ways, time and time again. Finally, I had the presence of mind to form a standard reply that went something like this, 'You know, you are correct. In this business you are going to have some theft. But, I've noticed that it is one of two kinds. It's either the canned corn or human dignity. I'm going with the canned corn!'

Amos claims the reason for KINSHIP's remarkable success is people power. They treat people as partners and peers, not problems or projects. "We draw near not to correct, fix, or cure them, but to know and be known by them. We draw near to discover that there is more to them than what, from a distance, defines them" (Dutney, 2005, p. 59). It upsets Amos to hear the people who come to them for help referred to as clients, or "opportunities for ministry." The "one essential, fixed, non-negotiable ingredient in our mix" is trusting and valuing people for who they are. Amos said. "There is no way to overestimate the importance and continuing impact of the community created by this attitude." Currently KINSHIP has about four hundred volunteers and 99% are people who also use the organization's services. "Talk about wealth," he said emphatically, " the collective and individual wisdom expressed by these people is amazing!"

KINSHIP has a written philosophy that serves as a guide for their decisions and a list of values that guide their behavior. Both are well developed and more extensive than it has been my experience to find in for-profit organizations. Of the thirteen published values, the number one value is love. It reads, "Love: We will treat each other and our neighbors with respect, dignity, and obvious love in every situation. The thirteenth value reads, "Courage: We will confront and challenge with 'tough love' anyone whose actions, words or decisions threaten the health of our community." Love and courage have taken KINSHIP beyond charity.

> Attempting to 'do good' can be dangerous and even harmful. Charity is often just a sophisticated way for people with power to maintain it. Charity puts the giver on top – and that's what's wrong. The 'poverty industry' has got the wrong mission. There is no reason for people to continue in the mess they are in. I am learning that the best response to people caught in poverty is to apply the Golden Rule, treat them like I'd want to be treated if I were in the same situation. Respect, mutual action, listening and organizing to change things out of a commitment to justice is the way to proceed. Real simple stuff—the Golden Rule—its not rocket science.

Athena the Communitarian gets up at 4:30 every morning to return emails. In response to my question why she is so diligent about quickly returning calls and emails (she gets 80 to 100 personal emails a day) she said,

97

"There is a human being behind every phone call or personal email. I try never to forget that. People are important and it's important that I acknowledge them as quickly as possible." I suggested that different cultures might view responding to email differently. She qualified her response. She doesn't respond or read emails that do not directly concern her or require a reply. But quickly added, "How ever they do it, I have to respond when people are trying to communicate with me."

Education

Education was a theme that repeatedly came up on several levels. First, there is the educational experience of each of the participants and how their growing awareness has shaped them. Second, educating others regarding the work of their organizations is vital and never stops. Whether it is donors, governmental agencies, politicians, business leaders, or neighbors—getting the message out is critical for accomplishing the mission. Third, educating the people who come to their organizations for services, and being educated *by* them, is the key to their ability to develop successful partnerships that work on solving real problems, versus perpetuating dependency on one side and paternalism on the other.

The participants are neither naïve or overly optimistic. They do not diminish challenges. Rather, they understand how important it is to understand and accurately read the cultural and political landscape. While working to change systems that are inherently oppressive or dysfunctional, they have learned how to work within those systems. Each participant's life shows a pattern of always learning, seeking new knowledge and understanding, in order to become more effective. Their leadership is continually evolving largely because of their ability to be open and reflective. When their assumptions are challenged, they think. They have made a habit of uncovering assumptions, both their own and those of others. A common assumption of some is that the poor are spiritually inferior. Amos said many Christians from the wealthy churches in his city feel a spiritual superiority toward the poor.

> For over ten years I have been witness to the humility, joy, courage, disappointment, resilience, creativity and deep spirituality of 'the poor.' It is the spirituality that gets me. The poor know the force back of the universe and their lives. Their brand of spirituality is surprising, unorthodox, uncluttered, practical, real, full of joy. When I made the decision to move my family into the inner city, friends from my old church said encouraging and complimentary things like, 'Oh, isn't it great! You are taking Jesus to the inner city.' My experience here teaches me that such a statement is so far from the truth as to be laughable! After less than a month it hit me: Jesus never left the city—the church, yes, but not Jesus. The follow up punch was even more enlightening: no one knows Jesus better than these people!

The city that is home to KINSHIP is one of the most highly churched cities in the nation. Many of these churches are tend toward Fundamentalism. Invariably, whenever Amos is visiting with religious leaders to talk about the work that KINSHIP is attempting to do, someone will raise the question of spirituality. They will ask him questions like, "So Amos, how do you evangelize as you do your work?" or "How do you address matters of the soul and spirit?"

> Underneath these questions, and often right out on the table for discussion is the idea that the real problem with poverty is a spiritual one. Thus, the real solution, the only remedy possible must be spiritual as well. I agree. The problem back of poverty in the United States today is most definitely spiritual. Poverty is a problem of the soul. But the problem isn't where they think it is.

A constant challenge for all three participants is educating those people who want to help, but whose help feels "an awful lot like judgment." The participants understand the necessity to challenge the thinking of those who oppose them on ideological or philosophical grounds. What is difficult, and often disheartening, according the Amynomene the Defender, are those friends, supporters, major donors and even Board members, "the people who are supposed to be on your side," who need to be educated. Working with well-meaning people who assume that because their intentions are good they cannot be elitist or racist is common. She said, "I realize we have to build a relationship and then educate them. They don't understand the poor and it's all about education."

Amynomeme participates on a committee of elected representatives, policy administrators, social sector leaders, and business people whose purpose is to address shelter and housing issues for the homeless in her city. She described a conversation that took place in one of the committee meetings in which she noted,

> Nearly 60% of the homeless in the city are people of color. But 70% of the available housing goes to whites. I said to them, 'Why is that? Could it be because the majority of people who have anything to do with housing are white? They reach out to their own but they don't know how to reach out to communities of color.' I said, 'Do you think that because I'm sitting at this table and I'm African American that all African Americans are going to hear about it [low-income housing]?' I said, 'More people of color would apply if they knew about it.' The Chairperson said, 'Well, it went out.' I said, 'To who?' She said, 'It went out through the regular channels.' I said, 'Do you assume that we are all plugged into your channels?' At that point, she got this patronizing tone—I hate it—and said, 'Well, yes, we should do something about that.' And she wanted to move on because she thought that would shut me up. But I said, 'What? What are we going to do about it?'

Amynomene claims she found "a way out" through education. She became a teacher and went on to get her doctorate in no small part due to the influence of several teachers in her life who showed they cared at critical junctures. They did not know the turmoil she was experiencing inside, how

100

horrible her circumstances were outside of the classroom, but each reached out to her, encouraged her and showed compassion. They treated her as if she were valuable in her own right, apart from homework assignments and classroom performance. She knows first hand what a vital role a teacher can play in fostering hope in a student simply by showing that they care.

I traveled to the State Capital with Amynomeme on a trip that HOME had organized for parents and children. The purpose of the trip was to advocate for several important legislative bills that would impact families in poverty. Amynomeme has made it a point to establish relationships with lawmakers. I watched as she skillfully and firmly negotiated with Senators and Representatives one minute, and then turned and invited each child into the conversation with the utmost respect and *expectation*. She asked children to step up, to express themselves in an environment that can be intimidating even for adults, and they did. They had social capital; they had teachers, parents, and peers. They knew they mattered to someone.

Justice and Social Justice

When the participants spoke about social justice versus justice, they were referring to social systems or institutions that privilege some at the expense of others. According to Novak (2002), most of the people who use the term social justice are not referring to an individual virtue, but to social systems. The focus is not virtue, but power, social *in*justice. Justice, on the other hand, is often treated like the virtue of an individual or a process. The terms justice and social justice show up frequently in the data so both terms are included. Justice is such a strong value in the lives of these leaders I began to wonder if there was a connection between their passionate commitment to justice, their hope, and their leadership? If so, what was it?"

Athena the Communitarian has been involved with social service work the longest of the three participants. She has been ED or CEO of three major social service nonprofit organizations, including the one she leads currently, Community Builders. "My biggest job has been coming into all white organizations and changing how people think about them," said Athena. She used to think you could solve a problem and it would stay solved forever. For instance, once you educate your board of directors and the staff regarding social justice issues you could move on to the next challenge. She has found social justice to be an on-going challenge even within the ranks of the people who claim to champion it.

> Any major institution has embedded racism if established and run by the racial majority. In order to be sure that your organization, the people within, are culturally aware and competent in a culturally relevant manner—you have to be very intentional about addressing institutionalized racism. People in the organization change. The board changes, so it's circular. It [the need to educate] goes on and on forever.

Amynomeme the Defender concurred that the challenges related to bias and inequity never end. She claimed she has been fighting individual racism and institutionalized racism her entire life and that she gets tired of educating well-meaning people who "just don't get it." Unfortunately, some of the people who don't get it are members of her own board of directors. Several years ago she suggested to her board of directors that the chairperson of HOME's Parent's Advisory Council be allowed to join the board. She reasoned having someone who could represent the parents would broaden the perspective of the mostly white board and would help them make more informed decisions. Their usually strong resistance surprised her. The unspoken implication was clear—a person who was homeless or formerly homeless had no place being at the table while the board discussed issues concerning homelessness and made important decisions. Amynomeme is both patient and persistent. Today, there are *two* people from the Parents Advisory Council serving on the board.

Frequently, she has observed, people of color do not get the same respect, the same air-space, in a group that is predominantly white. It feels normal to the dominant group so they remain insensitive. She pointed out to me that I had been a witness to this type of inequality and I did not notice it.

Amynomeme and I were part of a University cohort of twenty individuals who are some of the finest, most well-intentioned, and, as it turns out, often clueless, people I have ever known. Someone said, the fish is the last to know he's wet. Our cohort broke into small groups of three or four in order to do social justice projects as part of a service learning assignment. One group brought Tent City, a roving encampment of homeless people, to the University campus. The stated purpose of the organizers of Tent City is to raise awareness of the problem of homelessness. Tent City must move to a new location every few months and each move is often accompanied by a flurry of protests from neighbors who do not want the homeless anywhere near them. By bringing Tent City to campus, the University raised awareness concerning the problem of homelessness, set a charitable example, provided a learning opportunity for the students and faculty, and provided Tent City residents with a temporary place to stay. The students and faculty seized the opportunity to organize and participate in activities with Tent City residents and the event garnered mostly favorable publicity. The University considered it an overwhelming success.

Our cohort was self-congratulatory. In retrospect, one thing is striking about our cohort's process—we ignored the person in the room with the greatest expertise. Amynomeme has been working with the homeless her entire life. In our excitement, we never asked her what she thought during our discussions. Nor did we really *listen* when she asked provocative questions. When I think back, her questions should have raised our awareness concerning the deeper issues around homelessness, issues well beyond a campsite.

At first, she thought, "the cohort really cares about poverty and homelessness," and that she had "finally found a place where I can talk about these issues." She brought us some information about impending legislation that would have a serious negative impact on low-income families and the homeless. There was a desperate need for more opposition voices regarding the legislation. No one responded. She was invisible. She might as well have been talking about how to grow tomatoes. As she repeated this story to me, it instantly flashed in my memory and I thought, "Oh My God! She's right!" I asked her why she did not call us on our hypocrisy. She said,

> I've been fighting this all my academic life. People say we are social justice this and social justice that—and it was not that way at all. It was the same shit I was dealing with outside of the classroom. I said, I can't fight this in here too—I got to fight it out there. Being heard is a constant battle when it comes to oppression. There's battles everywhere—you just can't fight them all—you'd go crazy.

Amos the Prophet began his career as a Christian minister to the church. However, he has become a thorn in the side of organized religion in his city. He is quick to indict the hypocrisy of mainstream evangelical churches that provide a smattering of charity but refuse to look at the system that so often creates the need. He said that he is becoming more and more spiritual, and at the same time less and less religious in a traditional sense. He rails against self-justifying religions that divorce themselves from social problems.

> The folks caught up in that system of faith and thought found ingenious ways to neatly explain away human suffering and political injustice, while defending the status quo in pursuit of a rather narrow, self-serving, moralistic worldview. Would Jesus prop up a social system of injustice, unfairness and oppression?

He recalled a conversation with a religious leader who was the head of one of the most important foundations in the State. The man expressed his concern that nonprofits may be "losing their way" by abandoning more "traditional charity" for the work of community and economic development. Amos agreed that there was a "huge and demonstrable difference between charity and community development. Charity alone will never renew a neighborhood and will seldom change a life." After a long pause, the foundation leader changed the subject.

Amos thinks he may have stumbled upon part of the problem: the "take aways." Heifetz and Linsky (2002) agree, "People do not resist change, per se. People resist loss" (p11). Change represents loss. Who gains and who loses and what are they losing? We have the resources in the United States to end poverty in America. It might look like a technical challenge, but in reality it is an adaptive challenge (1994, Heifetz). Charity, on the other hand, does not threaten the status quo. Amos said donors love charity and that "helping people" is the most popular game in town.

> Charity is also a very nifty way for people with economic power to maintain control of that power while performing good work that often leads to their being recognized as good people in a community. Charity, on its own, seldom, if ever, challenges existing power structures, even when these power structures are responsible for much of the poverty being addressed by donor largesse. People with problems continue to present their 'issues.' People with money and, thus, power, maintain control of both, parceling it out at a rate keeping with their good judgment. At the same time they get a tax break for doing so.

In his city, large foundations seldom cooperate with one another to develop community-wide strategies for attacking poverty.

Foundations normally do not consult with community-based organizations to seek counsel on just how resources could best be allocated. Rather, the community groups usually try to figure out what foundations want to fund and then tailor requests in that direction. The unintended consequence of a good deal of charity is the creation of an unhealthy dependence among the poor on services that do not lead people out of their pressing need.

Amos lives in one of the wealthiest and most highly churched cities in the Nation. This Southern city has been described as socially conservative. Conversely, Amynomene and Athena live in the Northwest in one the least churched and most socially liberal cities in America. There is a palpable difference between these cities' attitudes toward poor.

However, Athena the Communitarian is quick to point out that even in a socially liberal city the charity impulse reigns when it comes to fighting poverty. Rescue is more popular than prevention. The more dramatic the rescue work the better donors feel. She said, "Funding preventative work, on the other hand, is always a challenge." Prior to the organization she currently leads, which is focused on preventing problems by strengthening families and community, she led an organization that sheltered and helped abused or neglected children.

People loved it when we told them what we did [at her previous organization]. We rescued children who were *under* the waterfall. They used to say, 'How wonderful! God bless you for what you are doing.' Now that I've moved upstream and am trying to prevent them from going *over* the waterfall in the first place—it's a lot harder to get funding. People don't get it right away and sometimes not at all.

The combined experience and wisdom of the three participants provided an eye-opening look at social service nonprofits and their often complex relationship to society in general. The longer I was with these leaders, the better I understood why they are so passionate about justice and why justice demands they be politically astute activists.

Compassion frequently demands confrontation.
—William Sloan Coffin

Amos the Prophet said, "Charity seeks to alleviate the effects of injustice, justice seeks to eliminate the causes of it." Amos described 3 levels in the work at KINSHIP that he has discerned over the years. Level 1 is the Good Samaritan.

> There was a guy who passed out on our steps one morning on a Sunday. I got here about 8 o'clock and he was laying there stretched out and I thought he was dead. He was just passed out. So we got him up, got him some breakfast, got him some coffee. He stayed for church. He had lunch. We stayed with him, ya know, in the Good Samaritan box we do the compassionate thing—you don't have any responsibility—all ya gotta do is breathe—you stay alive and we'll work with you. When we're doing this kind of work—people really applaud us—they love that. Back in those days we were still coming out of a suburban volunteer environment—and they loved that. I realized it was because *they were so needy themselves.* That kind of compassion is so tangible—I mean—the guys gonna die if you don't do something!

Level 2 is the getting involved, trying to help people reach some kind of sustainability or stability. It requires a deeper commitment than relief.

> We try to prepare people to play the game by the current rules. Things like a learning a workforce skill, addressing a medical issue that needs attention, or legal help in a domestic abuse situation. We're trying to get life stable where you can go. People like that too, business people like to see that. They get all jazzed because they see the potential of getting people in a position where they can sustain themselves.

Level 3 is taking on the system. Work at this level triggers the most opposition and requires the most courage.

The third level is the John 2 box, in which Jesus is kicking over the tables in the temple and clearing the place out. Questioning the rules. I mean we teach you to play by those rules even though some of those rules really are not right. We get involved in advocacy. Some people are uncomfortable when we do that—other people are attracted to us when we do that.

Those who wind up working for genuine renewal at the third level learn that renewal among the poor can become controversial, expensive and challenging, according to Amos. KINSHIP's renewal efforts, he said, "take us places we never have been before…with partnerships we never would have dreamed of!" They very quickly learned that success at this level is found in collaboration and community. Social capital is another theme woven throughout the data and is described later in this chapter.

Fear, Faith and Courage

Never befriend the oppressed unless
you are prepared to take on the oppressor.
—Ogden Nash

Fear, faith and courage were themes so intertwined, so dependent on one another, that they are treated as one theme. The projects the participants are involved with play a vital role in the lives of many people. The stakes are high. Heifetz and Linsky (2002) warned, "People push back when you disturb the personal and institutional equilibrium they know. And they resist in all kind of creative and unexpected ways that can get you taken out of the game: pushed aside, undermined, or eliminated" (p.2). All three participants referred to Dr. Martin Luther King Jr. as a personal role model. All three mentioned he was assassinated for opposing the status quo.

The participants are on the frontline challenging power structures that oppress vulnerable populations. Sometimes they are doing things that have never been done before, or things that *they* have never done before. Fear, anxiety, and self-doubt are regular companions. The burden of responsibility coupled with the enormity of the challenge can be overwhelming. Amynomene the Defender said she feels like she is "under siege."

> In my dreams I see this beach where I can finally rest. Will I ever get there? Will I make it? The beach—it's not in this country—I don't know where it is? I'm concerned I won't make it. I've got all this work to do that I can't put down. Every time I try to put it down it gets put in my lap again. I didn't ask for this but I can't put it down. (Pause) Maybe at some point I can stop being so frightened! (tears run down her cheeks—long pause) I don't know where that came from.

Athena the Communitarian notes that several years ago the idea was in vogue that CEO's and ED's should tell their Board of Directors their deepest fears.

> Tell them what keeps you up at night! Tell them so they can help you. And we all said, 'Are you nuts! They will use it against you.' On the other hand, you want to give the Board news in the context of the challenges the organization is facing. But I can't tell them, 'I'm so scared!' That doesn't engender their confidence in you. In a crisis it is a delicate balance to be absolutely truthful and yet not hopeless. I'm not always good at that. I remember in 2002, the year the bottom fell out of everything. We came out in the black. But, My God! It was a miracle.

Athena believes there no place for "magical thinking" if you want to survive a crisis. She said, " I buy a lottery ticket every week so I have some degree of optimism." On the other hand, she has learned to distrust overly optimistic reports. She said, "You've got to be careful when people love you too much." If all she hears is "wonderful this and wonderful that," she thinks, "What aren't they telling me?" She has found members of her board of directors are sometimes not prepared for the difficult challenges to which they have committed themselves, and sometimes prefer to remain in a state of denial. In 2002, her organization weathered a financial crisis.

There didn't seem to be any money anywhere, I remember waking up at 3:00 in the morning thinking I've got to figure out how to do this thing. I mean I am very practical. I know hard times when I see them. I tried to warn the Board. They said they wished I would be more optimistic. I said this is not the time to be optimistic. You need to know what the situation is. For me to come to you and say, I'm sure it is going to be OK—I'm not sure it's going to be OK.

Athena believes a leader must develop the capacity to face and endure conflict. Leadership itself is grounded in conflict as conflict unites as well as divides. Conflict, according to Burns (1978), "galvanizes, prods, motivates people" while "leadership acts as an inciting and triggering force in the conversion of conflicting demands, values, and the goals into significant behavior" (p. 39). Burns argued, "leaders, whatever their professions of harmony, do not shun conflict; they confront it, exploit it, and ultimately embody it" (p. 39).

Amos has learned that when the going gets tough—keep moving. He said, "Many of the dilemmas we've faced have brought us to the edge of a precipice. We've faced impossible odds, really hard problems with no discernable solutions. Against whatever odds or doubts, we just jump in." I ask, does he ever think, "I can't do this?"

Oh yeah! There are those dark moments in the middle of the night…I mean I have these incredibly horrifying gripping moments in the middle of the night where I am so full of doubt—self-doubt. (pause) I'm awake every night. I can't sleep. I got all kinds of self-doubt. But I can't live in that hole. It's just intolerable. And there is something about getting up the next day. You gotta fresh start. You just go at it. (pause) It's always better in the morning. Joy comes in the morning.

"Faith is simply moving *forward*…no matter what," according to Amos. Amynomene said, "We've got to make the impossible possible [for these kids]." Athena said, "I decide what I need to do, talk to whoever I need to talk to, and just get in motion." When faced with a fearful situation, the participants get all the information available, talk to everyone and anyone who will listen, and call in as many favors as they can. Their mixture of fear, faith, courage and hope is all about action. "Action is a declaration of faith," according to Novak (1978, p. 45.). "I've learned that real faith, in the real world, outside the theoretical, doesn't look much like what I was taught faith would look like. It looks a whole lot like really hard work...with lots of risk," said Amos.

> I flinch at success. There are always new questions...that come out of the fear. We work together and talk about it. Our questions are coming out of the fear—that's how we relate to one another—and the flinching and the answers are somehow provided by the dialogue in the community. If you didn't face it you would get run over, because it's not gonna wait. There are deadlines built into these processes and it's serious business and the world ain't stoppin' for the poor. So when you start to engage the system for the sake of people who don't have anything, they are gonna' try to run your butt over! They don't even know it. You talk about the whole principalities and powers thing...there is a force in the world that doesn't wait for the weak. It tries to destroy the weak.

With the stakes so high, the participants do not have the luxury to wait and see. While they are not always optimistic, they keep moving and never give up hope.

> *Hope is a state of mind independent of the state of the world.*
> *If your heart's full of hope, you can be persistent when you can't be optimistic.*
> *You can keep the faith despite the evidence, knowing that only in so doing*
> *has the evidence a chance of changing.*
> *—William Sloan Coffin*

The act of speaking out, taking action against injustice regardless of how daunting the opposition or improbable the odds affirms hope. Faith strengthens hope, according to Marcel (1962).

It consists in the affirmation that in hoping for liberation I really help to prepare the way for it, and that, inversely, in raising a doubt about its possibility I reduce the chance of it to some degree. It is not that strictly speaking I impute a causal efficacy to the fact of hoping or not hoping. The truth is much rather that I am conscious that when I hope I strengthen, and when I despair, or simply doubt, I weaken or let go of, a certain bond which unites me to the matter in question. This bond shows every evidence of being religious in essence. (p. 48)

Giving up hope is unthinkable. Despair is not an option for the participants, but they have learned they must stay connected. They repeatedly insisted that their hope is strengthened by their relationships, by their connection with people. Marcel (1962) asserted, "Hope is always associated with a communion, no matter how interior it may be. This is actually so true that one wonders if despair and solitude are not at bottom necessarily identical" (p. 58).

I chose public service nonprofit organizations for this study due to the seriousness of the challenges they face and, hence, the difficulty in maintaining hope. I thought keeping hope alive for the people who work in these organizations might be more difficult than in for profit organizations. I found the opposite. I found far more evidence hope and authentic engagement by the people in the three organizations that were part of this study than I have found in nearly forty years of working in the business sector. The people in these three organizations are able to cope with enormous human challenges because of their conviction regarding the meaningfulness of their mission and because of the relationships they forge. The most repeated word I heard from Amos was the word "amazing," always in reference to people.

We find constant hope in the surprising relationships we forge as we work together to fight poverty... Again and again, our poorest neighbors bring us strength, joy, creativity and courage. The people who struggle with poverty and against it continue to inspire us and move us forward.

112

While the participants described being occasionally depressed by obstacles and set backs, they do not stay depressed. One participant said, "I get knocked down a lot, but not defeated." Faith and conviction give them a firm grip on hope. "Hope is definitely not the same as optimism. It is not the conviction that something will turn out well, but the certainty that something makes sense, regardless of how it turns out," according to Vaclav Havel (1993, p. 68). Faith feeds hope and conviction gives hope its strength.

Amos the Prophet experienced an episode of depression recently in the midst of unprecedented growth and success. KINSHIP had battled prejudice, powerful opposition, bureaucratic hurdles, and lengthy negotiations with lawyers and business people, to finally close on an abandoned high-rise building in the center of the city. They are now in the middle of a major capital campaign in order to convert the building into a combination of market rate, low-income, and transitional housing for the homeless.

> The press of our unrelenting need for funding, the growing pains
> of our expanding organization, the number of high intensity
> projects now on the drawing boards, and the dramatic increase in
> the need in our community all combine in a way that wears me
> out!

Then, as usually happens to him when he gets depressed, he had a "break through" day. He said, "I found my life for work again—a literal surge of new energy, a clearing away of the fog from my soul. It happened when I listened, *really listened* to five guys who live on the street." This is his written account of what he heard that revived him.

> "I sleep on the street," William told us. "I cover up with my
> blankets. My blankets are precious to me because of the cold.
> One night last week, I woke up and realized there was another
> person under my blankets with me! A perfect stranger just trying
> to stay warm. He meant me no harm at all!"

> William told his story yesterday during one of our site visits by
> the United Way committee that will determine our funding level

for our housing efforts for the coming year. We met in the lobby of our recently acquired office building.

"The shelters don't allow us to store our belongings," Roger explained. "If we leave our stuff, they throw it away. What is precious to me, may not be to you, but it is to me!"

"If we look through the trash for what they throw away, they ban us from the shelters," William added. "We just need a place to leave our belongings, a place that is ours."

Three other gentlemen spoke —"Wild Bill," Leon and Troy. Like their other two friends, each was articulate, clear, honest, rational and impressive.

Leon told us that he was living in a shelter at present where everything was "beans and rice and Jesus Christ!" But he said he was glad for the bed, even though the shelter turned everyone out onto the streets at 5:00 a.m. every morning. He has a job, so it works for him. "But, what I really need is a place of my own," he added.

"Wild Bill" described his campground home. Troy told us about his struggle with drugs and life. When the men were done, we all sat in silence for a few moments before the committee's questions broke the silence. I think we all realized what great neighbors these five men would make. As I spoke with them afterwards, it was clear that the thought of a place of their own was beyond their ability to conceive at this point. The longer we visited, the more hopeful they became as I described apartments we would begin offering in May at another location in Dallas.

"Would the apartment be furnished?" Roger asked. When I told him that it would be, unless he wanted to use his own furniture, he just shook his head and said, "Do you know how long it has been since I slept on my own bed?"

William told the group during our formal presentation that one of the greatest needs of all is for simple privacy. "I'd like to be able to shut the door and take a shower or use the restroom. There is no privacy for any of us. "Every day we fall in line to join the 'parade' from place to place Downtown," Roger told us. "We need a place to call home where this can stop."

All the comments began when I asked these men the simple question, "What would an apartment of your own mean to you?" I came away more convinced than ever that most of us don't understand much at all about homeless people. Further, about all we need to understand is that they need a home, a place they can call their own. We're working on that right now.

When Amos is overcome with the enormity and seriousness of his work, he knows he cannot afford to dwell on the difficulty—he has got to keep moving—he has got to keep his purpose in mind and his purpose has many names—like William, Roger, Wild Bill, Leon and Troy. Amynomeme and Athena, likewise, keep moving in the face of enormous challenges. Of course, they are all *tempted* to despair, but when they get discouraged they have learned not to be seduced into a state of despair. They connect with the people who *re-mind* them of their purpose.

Authenticity

> *God does not float on the horizon,*
> *he sleeps in your substance.*
> *Vanity runs, love digs.*
> *If you fly away from yourself,*
> *your prison will run with you.*
> —*Gustave Thibon*

In existential philosophy, authenticity refers to "an emotionally appropriate, significant, purposive, and responsible mode of human life" (Soukhanov, 1992). The word authenticity itself refers to "reliability, dependability, trustworthiness, creditability; accuracy, truth, or veracity" (1992). The participants' stories reflect authentic lives full of purpose, freedom and responsibility, and commitment to truth.

Purpose

It was June 23, 1963. Her father forbids her to attend a march led by Dr. Martin Luther King Jr. She disobeys her father, even though she is afraid of him. She sees white people and black people holding hands, marching and singing together, something she has never seen before. She is captured by a vision that will shape her life. "I knew in my heart it was destiny speaking to me," recalls Amynomeme.

In the comfortable role of minister for a large, wealthy congregation, he reads a book, *Hunger for Justice: The Politics of Food and Faith* (Nelson, 1982), and Amos decides to change the course of his life and work with the poor. In making this choice, he is following this deepest calling, being true to his greatest possibility.

A ten-year-old middle-class white girl growing up in Mayberry, USA, reads *Angels in Hell's Kitchen* (McConnon, 1959). She determines then and there what she wants do with her life. She wants to help people build strong, loving communities. And she does.

All three participants are living out *their* story, appropriate to their possibilities, their potential and not that of another. Sometimes the stories people live out are pointless and meander, without seeming to have a connecting thread or set of threads (Novak, 1978). But even in the most purposeful lives it is not always clear to us where we are going. A friend of mine once said, "We are never present to the whole of our lives" (Ron Highfield, personal communication, 1997). While it may not have always been clear to the participants where they were going, their stories constitute a network of actions that have a strong connecting thread.

Freedom and Responsibility

In the concentration camp, this living laboratory…we witnessed some
of our comrades behave like swine while others behaved liked saints.
Man has both potentials within himself; which one is actualized
depends on decisions but not on conditions.
—Viktor Frankl

There will always be tension between our freedom and responsibility, both on a universal and on an individual level. Buber (1970) referred to an individual's freedom as "manifold." He said, "What is manifold is often frightening because it is not neat and simple. Men prefer to forget how many possibilities are open to them" (p. 9). Circumstances, all of the material things and forces outside of our control, impact our freedom and responsibility, making it difficult to perceive individual levels of each. We understand the assertion that all humans are *created equal* to mean they have the same right to dignity, to freedom of choice. Practically speaking, however, we do not experience an equality of freedom and responsibility.

The words authenticity, freedom, choice, responsibility, and accountability surfaced in the data repeatedly. On one level, the terms freedom and responsibility have to do with the kind of person we chose to be, regardless of external conditions. At another level, freedom and responsibility represent the liberty, resources and opportunities that are available to us. Factors like genetics, geography, class, gender, and race play a huge part in determining how much freedom and opportunity we experience. A third level has to do with whether or not a person has seized his or her potential as a human being, or fled from the "relentless demands of honesty, courage, freedom and community" (Novak, 1978, p.77).

In 2002, a comic-book hero leapt to the big screen in the movie *Spider-Man*. In one of the most repeated lines of the movie, Peter Parker has a

117

conversation with Uncle Ben, who councils, "Remember, with great power comes great responsibility." Privilege equals more power—more freedom and opportunity, and more responsibility.

"Freedom is social" (italics original, Novak, 1979, p. 126). The privileged do a further injustice to the least privileged when they assume the poor are somehow responsible for the condition in which they find themselves. Lack of health care, affordable housing, un-livable wages, unemployment and cycles of abuse are conditions in which the poor find themselves, they are not conditions chosen by poor people. "People can be very, very responsible and still be oppressed by unfair systems," according to Amos. He described feeling like he was under an incredible burden of privilege.

> I'm a white male. I've had all the advantages. I've had all the breaks…all the pathways cleared for me all my life. People say that's 'white guilt.' I say NO! It's not guilt. It's a burden of responsibility. It's seeing that much of what I received was probably at the expense of what others should have received.

He was free to choose a number of paths and he could have ignored the responsibility that comes with privilege. But he noticed that his values increasingly impinged upon his personal options. Eventually, he says, "I began to fall in love with my obligations." He found that religion, for some, served as a hedge protecting them from the radical nature of life's call to their true selves.

> I think I tried to be an evangelist for a long time before I finally faced the fact that I didn't believe anybody was lost. (laughs) It was kind of hard to be an evangelist when I found myself trying to soak up new knowledge from the people who I was supposed to be trying to convert…and found myself discovering all kinds of new truth in them. (pause) And then there are the *really* broken people. The ones who have been so badly abused I wonder at their level of responsibility in the whole grand scheme of things.

Amynomeme the Defender learned that accepting responsibility empowers. She understands the tension between showing unconditional love for a child and holding a child responsible for his or her choices. The children who attend school at HOME usually come with heartbreaking stories. They need a safe place and caring teachers. But, Amynomene said, "The white staff sometimes takes on this enabling role where they are too submissive and permissive." Teaching children to be responsible is critical for their survival. "This school is a bubble," she added. "Regardless of what they have been through or are going through, we've got to prepare them for what's out there. Otherwise they're gonna get their butts kicked." Teaching children to accept responsibility for their actions helps them survive. The goal in life is not to eliminate conflict but rather to act responsibly in the most difficult situations and to learn how to successfully with cope pain and suffering (Frankl, 1984).

Many of Amynomeme's male friends from childhood are in prison or dead. They became so demoralized they no longer saw a reason to finish high school, or try to improve their situation. They accepted the condition they found themselves in as hopeless.

> They was always talkin' about how the white man was puttin' em down and keepin' em down. They was always talkin' about 'the man.' I said one day, 'Well, Hell! If he's the man, who are you?' I was working and they were sitting on the porch saying 'the man' this and 'the man' that. I said, 'I'm tired of hearing about the man. I thought you were a man.' I realized, as I got older it had to do with not having hope—not thinking their lives were going to change—that it would be the same as their fathers and their fathers before them.

When confronted with a story of how someone successfully overcame enormous odds to lift himself out of poverty, I heard a young African American man say, "That's an inspiring story. But we can't all be poster boys. There's too many of us." Those of us with privilege have a responsibility to those without it. Amynomeme is all about helping people find hope by leveling the playing field.

Athena the Communitarian learned that no matter what her circumstances she had choices. She held a great deal of anger at a punitive supervisor early in her career. Then one day she just quit her job. "I realized how much time I'd spent focusing on how mad I was without realizing I had choices. I decided I didn't want to be mad, that I wanted a higher level of integrity." She began to imagine what she might do. In spite of the fact that all of her options had a downside, she realized she had many options.

> We always have choices. There are really very few times that we are absolutely victimized. Sometimes even a victimized person doesn't realize that he or she has choices. (pause) Then there are people who *really* have few choices in life, and there are a lot of those—for them that wouldn't be true at all.

People must be allowed to choose, said Amos. When KINSHIP tries to do *for* others the result is not so good. When they do *with* others the result is a growing sense of collective efficacy and social capital. This experience is supported by the research on motivation. Self-Determination Theory (Ryan and Deci, 2004) has identified three fundamental psychological needs for high self-esteem: (a) relatedness, (b) competence, and (c) autonomy. According to Ryan and Deci (2004), "acceptance without autonomy represents alienation" and "relatedness without competence represents amotivation and helplessness" (p. 476). Echoing the research, Amos claims that freedom of choice, and community are key determinants of health.

> People who feel as if they have no options, no power, no hope for progress, improvement of relief don't enjoy the same level of health and wellness as others who feel like they have more control over their lives. The absence of personal power and control likely explains, at least in part, the health outcome disparities between white and black Americans of the same socio-economic status in the United States.

Truth

Truthfulness is the foundation upon which trust is built. Trust is the lifeblood of nonprofit organizations, according to Jeavons (2005). The participants must be diligent to serve the organization's mission in a trustworthy

120

manner. Dependence on voluntary donors for funding makes maintaining public trust more critical for nonprofits than business or government. Any breach of ethics may have a dramatic effect on funding and the ability to pursue the mission. But trust goes well beyond the ability to secure funding. Trust is the fundamental principle upon which social capital grows. The participants stressed how much they depend on relationships built on trust. Trust fuels collective action. Trust is what allows them and their colleagues to be open and willing to share their experience and expertise with one another in order to pursue collective goals.

Athena the Communitarian is proud of the fact her colleagues at Community Builders openly disagree with her. One person told me that Athena sent her a note thanking her for "going toe-to-toe with me" in a large staff meeting. Athena said, "To say everything is fine when it isn't is disingenuous. Not facing the truth doesn't inspire hope—it inspires denial and mystical thinking and takes the power away from everybody. We've got to be able to talk about these things honestly."

Being truthful means being ethical. An ethics question given to Athena's 2002 leadership class at Stanford asked: If you have a large restricted grant, is it ever OK to spend it on something else? Athena answered, "Absolutely not!" However, 80 percent of her class thought it was OK. They rationalized money would come in from somewhere else that would cover the expenditure so that eventually money would be spent as designated.

Amos the Prophet gave an interview to a reporter from a local newspaper while I was shadowing him. Frankly, I was amazed by his candor. He did not *spin* the truth. He talked about KINSHIPS' weaknesses as well strengths. He answered all of the reporter's questions clearly and directly. It was a sharp contrast to the careful and vague, calculated and polished speech that many CEO's adopt when talking *to* the press. The reporter seemed to sense that more than a question and answer session was possible and the interview turned into an engaging dialogue. The reporter scheduled another visit the following week to delve deeper into the challenges faced by KINSHIP and the work they are doing. Amos told him, "Talk to anybody [in the organization] you want." Transparency at KINSHIP is deliberate.

Amynomeme the Defender said, "We don't pretend that something doesn't exist. We talk about it. If you are not telling the truth it will destroy your team." She added, "Sometimes telling the truth is painful, but it's more painful not to." One time her board of directors advised her to share the bad news concerning a financial crisis to the staff in phases. HOME would need to lay off several people but the board wanted to control the rate of the flow of information in order to "soften the news." They recommended that Amynomeme suggest to her staff the seriousness of the financial challenges facing HOME, wait a few weeks for the staff to accept the idea, and then do the layoffs. Amynomeme was adamant, "No! We've got to lay it out now. We've got to tell it now or nobody will ever trust us again!" She explained that the African American culture prefers truth before peace, while other cultures prefer peace or harmony before truth. She argued that there could be no *real* peace or harmony for all people until we face the truth. She noted that sometimes the strongest voices calling for peace over truth are the voices of the most powerful.

In different ways, each participant said truthfulness, or honesty, was essential for authenticity and the development of real hope. Amos added, "People cannot accept truth and health and hope and life until they face the lies, the illness, the despair and the death that grips them."

Mission

The key to the participants' effectiveness in their leadership roles is their personal alignment, or congruency, with their organization's purpose. The story of each of their lives fit the missions of the nonprofit organizations in which they serve as leaders.

The mission of KINSHIP is unapologetically religious: "To share the love of God by building genuine community in the neighborhoods where we live and work." Amos is a man of God. However, the way in which I understand him to conceive of God would shock the church going population of his city. His "ultimate concern" (Tillich, 2000) is *much* bigger, *much* more life affirming, and *much* less destructive than God defined by dogma. Gordon Allport (Allport as cited in Halling, 2000) observed that people who attend worship services regularly tend to be more prejudiced than those who do not, but that there were "a minority of religious people who are more tolerant than either their religious compatriots or most who are not involved in religion" (p.147). Amos is more than tolerant of those who are different; he is an outspoken critic of intolerance and religious hypocrisy.

Amos fulfills the function of a Biblical prophet to a comfortable, wealthy society that is overly impressed with its own righteousness. But he is more than a prophet or activist. He is a husband, father, grandfather, friend, and neighbor. He is also a sports fan and a bit of a jock. Like many highly intelligent people, he is complicated. He is driven by a compassion for people, which fuels his passion for justice. He cannot be true to himself and turn away from those who are suffering, struggling, and oppressed. Love demands justice. I asked one of his co-workers what the leadership was like at KINSHIP. He said, "It's like an intelligent goodness." That is what drives Amos and this organization.

The mission of HOME is to educate and nurture children whose families struggle with the risk or reality of homelessness. As only someone who has experienced childhood trauma can, Amynomeme the Defender understands children in crisis have special needs. In addition to helping children, HOME offers housing and support services that enable families to achieve stability. Amynomeme survived a childhood of racism and prolonged sexual abuse to become an inspired and inspiring leader. "Helping others overcome pain is something I am very familiar with… It took me a long time to heal from the inside out—by embracing the pain I find my strength. I am driven to do what I do," she said. She refers to herself as "an old warrior." I am reminded of a Vietnamese proverb that asks, "How many indifferent men [women] are equal to one man [woman] of courage and determination" (Novak, 1979, p. 52)? Amynomeme, the Amazon warrior in Greek Mythology whose name means Blameless Defender, is an apt pseudonym for her.

The mission of Community Builders is to strengthen families and build caring, confident youth and future leaders. Athena the Communitarian loves community. After a long, and sometimes tense, meeting that involved multiple constituencies was concluded, Athena commented cheerfully, "Isn't it great how we got everybody involved in this process!" She grew up an only child, but her mother reports there was nothing she liked better than getting the neighbors all together. When cousins and relatives would visit, she was thrilled. While I shadowed her, I was struck by the specific and perceptive appreciation she expressed to many different people. Her skill at drawing others into the conversation was immediately apparent. Her clear strength is recognizing and utilizing the talents of others and forming collaborations. Athena, the Greek goddess of wisdom associated with mentoring heroes as well as strategy and tactics in battle, is a perfect pseudonym for her, and the mission of Community Builders is an excellent match for her passion and strengths.

The participants' choices and actions constitute the stories they are living out, but choice and action are not everything. Grace plays a part. Their willingness to take a step is often met with unexpected grace. None of the participants foresaw where they would be today. Novak (1979) observed,

What we did not want at first, would never have chosen, turns
out to be the best thing that happens to us in that decade. We
don't recognize our own motives for taking up a line of work,
but the years gradually reveal to us that we were led by obscure
instincts in making each unreflective choice, whose correctness
we never could have guessed. So many of the best, deepest, and
most important turns in our lives were not exactly of our own
choosing, certainly did not spring from careful analysis, but
came as gifts… (p. 59)

While the participants did not set out to be leaders, neither did they
accidentally *drift* into positions of leadership. They are on a mission. It is a
mission for others and with others.

Social Capital

The evocative title of Robert D. Putnam's book, *Bowling Alone: The
Collapse and Revival of American Community* (2000), telegraphs a fact
experienced by many people; Americans are becoming more individualistic and
isolated from each other. Putnam makes a distinction between several kinds of
capital. Physical capital refers to physical objects. Human capital refers to the
properties of individuals. Social capital consists of communities built on trust
and commitment. According to Putnam (2000),

Social capital refers to connections among individuals — social
networks and the norms of reciprocity and trustworthiness that
arise from them. In that sense social capital is closely related to
what some have called 'civic virtue.' The difference is that
'social capital' calls attention to the fact that civic virtue is most
powerful when embedded in a dense of network of reciprocal
social relations. A society of many virtuous but isolated
individuals is not necessarily rich in social capital. (p. 19)

Social capital in the context of this study relates to the social capital of
the participants within the broader community upon which they depend for
funding and also to the social capital they work to create in the vulnerable

populations their organizations serve. First, as nonprofit leaders, their power and influence in the broader community is not derived from social position or wealth. Their social capital is a direct reflection of their perceived credibility and trustworthiness (Jeavons, 2005).

Amynomeme the Defender knows the value of showing up. In spite of a grueling schedule, she rarely says no to a request to speak at a Rotary luncheon, to a K-12th grade class or university class, or at a conference. In addition to her frequent trips to the State Capital, she makes several trips a year to Washington D.C. to speak on issues involving equity and justice that impact the poor and disenfranchised. She is able to carry out her public role, to be the face of HOME in the community, because of the support of her colleagues. One of her colleagues told me, "I wanted to work here because of Amynomeme. At first I volunteered, then I caught the spirit of this place [HOME]. It's her spirit. We need to be here making it [HOME] run so she can be out there—telling the story."

Athena the Communitarian frequently spoke of the importance of building alliances. She is a founding member of a nonprofit organization whose purpose is to build social capital among nonprofits and foundations in the region. She is also a member of a peer group that has been meeting for six years. "They are FABULOUS women," she enthused. "Our conversations are confidential. There is total trust and we meet once a month without fail." They bounce ideas of off each other, share information regarding the political landscape, and offer personal support. "I can't imagine how much more difficult my life would be without the support of this group," she claimed.

Athena described herself as "very political." She said, "Politics has a bad sound to it but it is really just assessing the landscape and understanding what piece of it you need to be active in." She frequently used strategy and tactical thinking metaphors while conversing with her colleagues while I was shadowing her. She emphasized whom they need to build strong relationships with in order to get things done. At her initiation, Community Builders collaborates with several other nonprofit organizations. She is not the least bit concerned about who gets the credit as long as the work gets done. She added, "What we really need to do is change the system—because it just sucks!"

Amos the Prophet and KINSHIP want to change the system as well. Together, people can change systems. Social capital creates a sense of validation, of meaning in our lives. According to Amos,

> My behavior, my genetics, my community has a lot more to do with my health than my doctor. But *access* to the doctor says something about my value. I am not disposable. I support universal health care because of what it says about the worth of a human being. [pause] We're spending 15% of our gross domestic product on health care, which is more than any developed nation…and we have the worst outcomes! We are all focused on individual health instead of community health.

Research that supports the connection between social capital and health is growing, according to Putnam (2000).

> The networks that constitute social capital also serve as conduits for the flow of information that facilitates achieving our goals… Social capital also operates through psychological and biological processes to improve individual's lives. Mounting evidence suggests that people whose lives are rich in social capital cope better with traumas and fight illness more effectively… Community connectedness is not just about warm fuzzy tales of civic triumph. In measurable and well-documented ways, social capital makes an enormous difference in our lives. (p. 289)

The more my existence includes others, according to Marcel, the more I am (1951/1996). "Hope is always centered on a *we*, on a living relationship and if we have not noticed this fact it is because we too often use the word hope when what is at issue is in fact [individual] desire" (p. 608). The importance of a caring community for hope cannot be overestimated. "Hope is fostered in relationships where individuals are reminded that they matter to others and

where they learn that they are worthy of being heard" (Larsen, Edey, and
LeMay, 2005, p. 515). Social capital, community, commitment, relationship,
often forged in connection with the pain of others, was a source of love, joy,
hope and meaning for the participants.

Leadership

Too much sanity may be madness! But maddest of all—
to see life as it is and not as it should be.
—*Don Quixote*

The participants were asked to describe what leadership meant to them.
Amynomeme the Defender described leadership has an unintended consequence
of a decision to take action on something that matters.

> I think leadership—for me—it's not about, 'Are people following
> me?' I am always amazed when I find there are others behind
> me—cause I don't start out like that. I start out with, 'Is this
> something that needs to happen and I start looking for ways to
> make it happen.'

One of her colleagues described Amynomeme as "visionary, incredibly
powerful—not in a crude way, but a creative way. It's her spirit that everything
here is based on—generous, soulful, deeply kind, impish." Amynomeme did not
set out to become a leader, but she has attracted an awful lot of followers who
want to go in the direction she is headed.

Athena the Communitarian believes leadership is about encouraging
other people to be authentic. While being visionary is part of leadership, she
claims that her skill as a leader has more to do with bringing out the best in
others.

Leadership is about encouraging people to be all that they can be so the organization can be all that it can be. But I really can't say what that invisible thing is that leaders have. But I think that they are authentic, smart, competent, can think on their feet, can think of complex issues, and divide it into chunks so they can manage it. And they generally have good people skills, but you can be a strong leader for all the wrong reasons.

Athena believes a sound mission comes first. People and resources will be attracted to the mission if it truly serves the community. She described one of her greatest leadership lessons as learning to stop "social working problem employees" and focus on improving the ability of the organization to fulfill the mission. She finally came up with an orientation for new employees that she has recited so often that everyone in the organization can recite it to each other.

I will go to the mat for you 100% of the time, *except* for the time when what you need differs from the needs of Community Builders. My job is to be sure that Community Builders is above reproach, healthy, and going forward. If your needs interfere with that—Community Builders comes first.

Amos the Prophet spoke of leadership as being the capacity to envision a reality before it is a reality. It is about having enough faith to move against obstacles and barriers not because what is envisioned is probable, but because it is possible.

Leadership is putting legs on vision. Leadership is the magic portion. It's never resident in one person even as it is happening. But it's kind of—it creates a wake, a movement, that literally puts the capacity to advance a vision. It's all about movement and persuasion.

It is also about having enough humility to accept something you never thought of originally because the vision always changes. You have got to be flexible because leadership is *literally* movement, according to Amos.

What I mean is you are bringing people along with you freely. You are not imposing. You are not dictating. You ARE persuading. You are hopefully enlightening and all while you got the back door open, or the side doors open, or the hatch open, to receive, new direction—new understanding from anybody and everybody.

This kind of openness in leadership requires faith. "It means I don't get to be in control, feel in control, or act like I even know what control means," laughed Amos. His attitude flies in the face of a culture that insists a leader always has a plan, always knows what is going on and is always in control. "That's just ridiculous!" he commented. "Better to surround yourself with trusted advisors, listen to the community, work together and *stay flexible*."

Athena the Communitarian said, "I learned very quickly how important it is to have trusted advisors." She surrounds herself with really bright, competent people and then listens to them. "No matter how bright or passionate you are, nobody knows it all. If you set yourself up to be the smartest one in the room you eventually go down the drain," she said.

Amynomeme the Defender emphasized how important it is to listen to *all* voices. One of her strengths, I observed, is her ability to bring attention to the small voices in the group that the group does not always recognize. Also, when soliciting participation from people who might be reluctant to participate she was careful how she framed the invitation. For instance, she reached out to parents and invited them to come to a "gathering" as opposed to a "meeting." Instead of saying, "We want your help," which sounds a lot like work, she said, "We want your good thinking."

Ryan and Deci's Self-Determination Theory (2004) was not referred to specifically by the participants, but the importance of creating a workplace that fosters autonomy, competence and relatedness, in order for people to be highly motivated, surfaced throughout the interviews. Each participant stressed how important it was for the organization to match the right people with the right position, along with giving them a sense of ownership in their work. Speaking of a highly talented co-worker who was in a position ill-suited to his strengths, Amos said, "We need to create a place where he can be wildly successful. We owe it to him—and us—he's just too valuable."

The participants exhibited and/or spoke of many leadership traits such as modeling, political savvy, conflict resolution skills, the ability to articulate a vision, and coalition building. But more than anything else, they stressed the importance of telling the truth. Truth is essential for the survival of trust and trust is essential for hope. "Facing the worst possible scenario can be liberating," said Amos. "It is when we have nothing to lose that we are the most emboldened."

Leadership and Hope

Recall that according to Snyder (2000a), "Hope is the sum of perceived capabilities to produce routes to desired goals, along with the perceived motivation to use those routes," (italics original, p. 8). This is a refined version of an earlier definition in which hope is described as clearly defined goals, plus waypower thinking (agency or the ability to determine pathways to reach those goals) and willpower thinking (the motivation to pursue those goals) (Snyder, 1994; Snyder, McDermott, Cook, & Rapoff, 1997). I gave Amos a printed description of Snyder's definition of hope that included a description of each of the components. Without telling him what I thought about it, I asked him to read it and then tell me his thoughts. Did he find the definition useful? He said,

> What's missing (pause) what's wrong with this (long pause) it
> assumes that hope is an individualistic trait. And hope is not
> sustainable as (We are interrupted by someone who walks into
> his office to ask him a question. He answers then looks back at
> the sheet of paper). Goals are the easy part! Seeing what ought to
> happen is the easy part. The harder part is the willpower and

waypower (pause) but even when we're talking about my individual passion it is fueled by the people around me and the opponents I face. (pause) You're in a battle where the goals are clear and they are really right, but the community of power stands over and against you. You've got the motivation, the passion, but you run into obstacles that have got to be cleared out of the way—someone has to help you make a way. I might combine my vision and willpower with John's waypower. (pause) Nobody does it alone. And the recognition that you can't achieve alone is one of the prerequisites for authentic community. (pause) I mean (pause) I don't even talk about self-efficacy. I don't think that way. It's about collective efficacy—social capital. Collective efficacy is *really, really, really* important for the creation of an atmosphere of hope. (pause) Hopes got to have a culture in which to grow. It can't just be in me. I'm too little.

The participants understand that great things happen only when the talent and energy of many people is unleashed, when individuals are willing to join others in commitment to a common purpose. Conflict is used to galvanize the community. Gardner (1990) said, "People talk of the legendary leader 'you would follow over a cliff,' not mentioning that it happens only when those following are deeply committed to something the leader symbolizes" (p. 187). Followers are attracted to the values that Amos, Amynomeme, and Athena symbolize.

Summary and Conclusions

The participants' stories reflect the experience and beliefs of three very real human beings who are examples of values-driven leadership. I selected leaders who had a track record of excellence because I believed it would be unethical to deliberately select someone to participant in this study whom I believed to be a bad leader, gain their trust, and then use them as an example of what leaders should not to do. I had good reason to believe that the participants selected were good leaders. However, in analyzing the data it struck me that the

132

portrait of these leaders was *too* good. Their portraits sounded like another heroic conceptualization of leadership.

Nonprofit organizations, Drucker (1990) warned, "…are prone to consider everything they do to be righteous and moral and to serve a cause" (p.11). I was concerned that I was romanticizing the data. After all, I constructed the map of the participants' experience of leadership and hope, I selected the highway markers, chose the historical and scenic points of interest. I wondered if I was seeing what I wanted to see. I went back through the data many times, rearranging information, questioning whether I had identified and labeled the themes correctly. When I let the data speak for itself, the congruency between the participants' values and their actions was unmistakable. It was clear the participants were people of integrity. Then the thought struck me, has integrity become so rare in positions of leadership that I construe it as heroic?

> *Don't call us saints.*
> *We don't want to be dismissed that easily.*
> *—Dorothy Day*

The participants do not see themselves as heroic. I witnessed how uncomfortable they became when people agreed with them too quickly. They deflected praise and compliments as if avoiding a bear trap. These are not perfect people. They make mistakes, misread situations, say the wrong thing, do the wrong thing, over react, under react, are inconsistent and more—but they do all these things without guile. They have integrity. While I thought I needed to find some discrepancies between their espoused beliefs and their actual behavior, I was stepping over the biggest reason that others so willingly join them in collective action. The key finding in the data was the alignment of their values with their behavior—their integrity.

If integrity, authenticity, or congruency between their values and their behavior was key to their success as leaders, how did it happen? I then arranged the dominant themes according to what I thought might develop first in order for the subsequent themes to develop. The result is *somewhat* of a developmental order of the dominant themes: (a) personal values, (b) education, (c) justice and social justice, (d) fear, faith, and courage, (e) authenticity, (f) mission, (g) social capital, and (h) leadership.

The development of Amos, Athena, and Amynomeme's intergrity, or authenticity, is a result of a series of choices they made over the course of their lives, influenced by factors such as genetics, experience, and education. Lives are created through our choices and it is the recognition of our freedom and responsibility that allows us to create meaningful lives (Block, 1998). The compassion they felt for people resulted in an expanding awareness of inequity and injustice which led to a growing passion for justice. The tension between their freedom and responsibility, the awareness of the inconsistency between their deeply held values and their actions, forced them to make choices throughout their lives that would allow them to either become more authentic or less authentic. They could have chosen to dissemble their true feelings and beliefs related to their values, becoming inauthentic. They could have submerged, denied, compartmentalized, rationalized or ignored their compassion for people, their deeply held belief that love demands justice. Or, they could begin to act on their values in accordance with their beliefs. As they chose to align their actions with their beliefs, they stepped out in faith, faith in action became courage (hope). They attracted people who shared their values (social capital), resulting in the development of relationships built on hope and leadership in the service of a common purpose.

The most interesting aspect of this conceptual framework is that leadership for its own sake is meaningless; it was never the end-goal, and means nothing to the participants apart from its utility in supporting their values. Yet, how comfortable is our post-modern world at acknowledging the role that values play in leadership? Many leadership studies programs proudly claim to be "value free." How is that even possible? The leadership of the participants is successful precisely because it is value saturated. Integrity, virtue and community are the foundation of the leadership of the participants. These themes will be developed more in the final chapter.

Theoretical Framework

A cognitive model of hope (Snyder, 2000a) focused on individual achievement proved to be inappropriate and/or insufficient for a phenomenological study. The participants' stories and actions throughout the data gathering process continually reinforced the multi-dimensional and relational nature of hope. Fortunately, I had two theoretical guides going into this study.

The broadest theoretical underpinning came from the philosophical themes of existentialism and was suggested by the theoretical perspectives on hope outlined in *Hope and Hopelessness: Critical Clinical Constructs* (Farran, Herth, & Popovich, 1995). The authors suggest hopes' experiential, spiritual, relational and rational attributes are supported by existential literature from psychology, philosophy and theology. According to Jevne (2005), Farran, Herth, and Popovich made an effort to integrate the many dimensions of hope by suggesting that,

> Hope can be expressed as a way of feeling (affectively), as a way of thinking (cognitively) and as a way of behaving and relating (behaviorally). They ventured to consider 'the experiential process as the *pain* of hope, the transcendent or spiritual process

135

as the *soul* of hope, the rational process as the *mind* of hope and the relational process as the *heart* of hope.' (p. 266)

In hindsight, it is not surprising that the existential theoretical guide proved more appropriate for a phenomenological study as phenomenology itself is rooted in existentialism.

Finding Hope

Amos, Amynomeme, and Athena's hope is strengthened in connection with others. Ronna Fay Jevne (2005) was closest to the truth of what the participants have discovered in working with vulnerable populations. Jevne was appointed the Head of Psychology in a cancer center at a time she described as, "when physicians *owned* patients"(p. 272). She did not relish navigating the political potholes and resistance she would face and considered quitting. Instead she crafted a vision of the future, "where a whole universe of caring people understood that nothing is as therapeutic as recognizing the pain [of others]… a community of people who believe—who believe that caring makes a difference" (2005, p. 272). Caring—compassion—love has made all the difference in the lives of the Amos, Amynomeme, and Athena. Love has allowed them to connect with the others in concrete ways that help them transcend the pain of circumstance to find hope and meaning.

While leaders may inspire and encourage hope, the statement, "The first and last task of a leader is to keep hope alive," (Gardner, 1968, p. 134.), understood literally, puts too much emphasis on the part of the leader. According to Amos, "Hope is already there [in community]. It's in the connection that hope is kept alive. You just have to connect." Jevne concurs (2005), "Hope is not something I do for you. It is a place where I meet you" (p. 281).

136

CHAPTER FIVE

CONCLUSIONS AND RECOMMENDATIONS

This study sought to develop a better understanding of how hope functions within the performance of leadership. Three leaders of nonprofit social service organizations were shadowed for a period of 3-4 days each while they performed their professional duties. An existential phenomenological perspective provided the theoretical foundation for the study. Data were collected from observation, in-depth interviews, and document analysis. The method of analysis was grounded theory (Glaser and Strauss, 1967). Patterns that emerged from the data were sorted, identified, and categorized into eight dominant themes: (a) personal values, (b) education, (c) justice and social justice, (d) fear, faith, and courage, (e) authenticity, (f) mission, (g) social capital, and (h) leadership. The participants' stories reflected a commitment to truth, purpose, freedom and responsibility—a striving for authenticity. Data revealed that altruistic love was a primary motivation for these leaders. The personal values of the participants led to choices that have resulted in the development of authentic leadership in the service of a social purpose. This study suggests that hope is kept alive through caring relationships and that, for these leaders, hope primarily functions as the virtue of courage in community.

Summary of Findings

The participants' stories suggest that leadership is a by-product of their personal integrity. In analyzing the data, it struck me at first that the portrait that I was developing of these leaders was *too good*. Their portraits sounded like another heroic conceptualization of leadership. I kept thinking I needed to find some discrepancies between their espoused beliefs and their actual behavior.

Then I realized that the key component of the data were their values and the alignment of their values with their behavior.

If personal authenticity and congruency between values and behavior, or integrity, was the key to their success as leaders, how did it happen? I arranged and linked the dominant themes developmentally in retelling the participants' stories. The themes are not ordered in a strictly linear progression, but do represent stages of growth, or personal breakthroughs. Additionally, the themes work together synergistically. The dominant themes are: (a) personal values, (b) education, (c) justice and social justice, (d) fear, faith, and courage, (e) authenticity, (f) mission, (g) social capital, and (h) leadership.

A suggestion for how the themes relate to one another is made in this brief conceptual framework. The participants' values have been developed through experience, education and their choices. At various points in their lives, their values, especially their compassion and high value in which they held human life, coupled with their sense of equity, collided with the injustice they witnessed in the world. The discrepancy between their worldviews and actions resulted in a high level of cognitive dissonance. They were forced to make a choice. They could submerge, deny, compartmentalize, rationalize, scapegoat, project, or employ some other method of self-deception regarding their awareness of injustice, or begin to act on their values in accordance with their beliefs. To be authentic, their compassion and love for people demanded a response—they would have to accept both their possibility and responsibility, while rejecting easy or comfortable rationalizations/accomodations. It required they grapple with fear and self-doubt. They took a leap of faith. Faith in action became courage (hope). Connection with others who shared their values (social capital) led them to engage in the activity of leadership on behalf of others. Leadership is a by-product of their integrity.

To become a leader was never a goal for the participants. Their leadership is a consequence, a result, of the pursuit of a personally meaningful life. Although many leadership programs assert that they are "value free," the leadership of the participants is successful precisely because it is value saturated.

What Did Not Work

Two theoretical frameworks guided this study, one was more suitable than the other. The existential phenomenological framework was highly abstract. Hope Theory was more particular, involved a low level of abstraction, and operationalized hope. According to Snyder (2000a), "*Hope is the sum of perceived capabilities to produce routes to desired goals, along with the perceived motivation to use those routes,*" (italics original, p. 8). An earlier definition described hope as *clearly defined goals*, plus *waypower thinking* (agency or the ability to determine pathways to reach goals) and *willpower thinking* or the motivation to pursue goals (Snyder, 1994; Snyder, McDermott, Cook, & Rapoff, 1997). I suggested that hope was like a three-legged stool that consists of goals + willpower + waypower. With this definition, I thought I had found a model, which could be applied in the performance of leadership within organizations, to manage the level of hope. Hope Theory could be used as a diagnostic framework, based upon demonstrable facts, to make hope more predictable within the organization. However, I found the participants acted on faith, not facts. They *used* facts, but facts were not the basis for their hope. Rather, their hope was based upon conviction, faith, love, imagination, community and courage.

I did not anticipate the problems I would encounter in my attempt to apply a quantitatively-oriented theoretical construct (Hope Theory), focused on individual achievement, to a qualitative study of a social phenomena, focused on collective achievement (leadership). According Glaser and Strauss (1967), a pivotal belief…of most social scientists is that through the processes of verification and quantification, social phenomena may be reduced to those 'primary qualities' of an 'absolute and objective' reality. Glaser and Strauss contend that this can be accomplished only through avoiding one of the most potentially confounding variables: the immediate context of the everyday world of people." (Glaser and Strauss as cited by Lewis, 1992, p. 286)

Leadership is a social phenomenon; it is a relationship. It is always experienced in a social context involving more than one individual. The participants' stories, their examples of hope, *all* began with connection. Marcel claimed, "Hope is always associated with a communion, no matter how interior it may be. This is actually so true that one wonders if despair and solitude are not at bottom necessarily identical" (1962, p. 58). An individualistic, achievement-oriented definition of hope proved to be too narrow for this study.

What Did Work

The broadest theoretical underpinning came from the philosophical themes of existentialism and was suggested by the theoretical perspectives on hope outlined in *Hope and Hopelessness: Critical Clinical Constructs* (Farran, Herth, & Popovich, 1995). Existential themes such as suffering, despair, freedom and accountability are precursors to finding hope and meaning. The themes of fear, courage, authenticity, freedom and responsibility, as well as faith, hope, and love, are unmistakable in the data. Hopes' experiential, spiritual, relational and rational attributes are supported by this study, as well as by existential literature from psychology, philosophy and theology (Farran, Herth, & Popovich, 1995).

Conclusions

This study was inspired by John W. Gardner's oft-repeated phrase; "The first and last task of a leader is to keep hope alive" (1968, p. 134). Gardner's statement, understood literally, contains two assumptions; (a) leaders are in some way responsible for the hope of others, and (b) leaders are capable of keeping hope alive or allowing it die. If true, in what way, and to what extent, is a leader responsible for the hope of others? How do leaders perceive and fulfill that responsibility?

This study indicates that Gardner's statement should not be interpreted egocentrically on the part of a leader, as if it is the leader's task (work) to manage the hope of others—the word for that is manipulation. While leaders may inspire and encourage hope, this statement, taken literally, puts too much emphasis on the role of the leader. Hope is found in community. Hope is kept alive through genuine connection in caring relationships. "Hope is not something I do for you. It is a place where I meet you" (Jevne, 2005, p. 281).

Gardner (1990) called attention to the "issues behind the issues" in leadership, which he identified as motivation, values, social cohesion and renewal (p. xvii). This study suggests that how leaders diminish or enhance the hope of others has more to do whether or not, and how well, they address these issues than with their intelligence, charisma, leadership skills, and technical competence. Gardner advocated values led commitment and accountability based on the obligations and duty that come with freedom and privilege. Leadership under this framework requires virtue, especially the virtue of courage. Gardner's masterpiece, *On Leadership* (1990), stressed the importance of finding common ground and restoring community. Values led leadership is not a position, nor is it sought solely for status, power or privilege. Rather, it is experienced as a responsibility of privilege and a commitment to welfare of the community.

Leadership that challenges hypocrisy and the status quo, works for the common good, and fosters the "release of human possibilities" (Gardner, 1990, p. 122) describes the leadership of the participants of this study. These leaders find hope in community. A deep reverence for life and compassion for people is their primary motivation. In the case of these leaders, faith proceeds hope—faith in the meaningfulness of caring for others, fighting poverty and oppression, providing opportunity, protecting and building community. Hope, then, acts as the virtue of courage, giving the participants the ability to move forward with others on behalf of others.

Virtue

> Love without courage and wisdom is sentimentality,
> as with the ordinary church member.
> Courage without love and wisdom is foolhardiness,
> as with the ordinary soldier.
> Wisdom without courage and love is cowardice,
> as with the ordinary intellectual.
> But the one who has love, courage and wisdom
> moves the world.
> —Ammon Hennacy

Virtue is the undercurrent in the stories of Amos, Amynomene, and Athena. They would often commit themselves to a project because it was the right thing to do, without knowing how, or if, they would succeed. Their stories reveal that as they made themselves vulnerable and embraced the pain of others they found meaning and purpose. As they stepped out in faith, were joined by others, ideas and efforts were met with new resources, new ideas, new directions, new allies, as well as new enemies and obstacles. Their hope is based on why, not how. "It [hope] is not the conviction that something will turn out well, but the certainty that it makes sense, regardless of how it turns out," (Havel, 1993, p. 68).

142

Virtue is "moral excellence" or "to conform one's life to ethical principles" (Soukhanov, 1992). Values are not the same as virtues. Personal values evolve from experience with the external world, may change over time, and are implicitly related to our personal choices. A person may value honesty because they have found that it is more expedient to be honest than dishonest. But honesty functions as a virtue, a moral character strength, only when it is a *commitment* to be truthful, regardless of the utility or the consequences. It takes courage to be a truthful person. But authenticity *depends* upon being truthful.

The virtue of courage depends upon justice to be a real virtue. Courage often evokes images of heroic acts of bravery in the face of danger. But the virtue of courage, especially in leadership, is less about bravery and self-confidence in an extraordinary circumstance than it is about truthfulness, steadfastness and patience in facing the challenges of daily life. The leader who has developed the virtue of courage is willing to be vulnerable, to endure wounds and make sacrifices for the sake of the common good. Putting oneself in harm's way uncritically and indiscriminately is not courage. Real courage requires a correct appreciation of reality, an awareness of our substantial vulnerability, and a commitment to live according to our values regardless of the personal cost. Courage is a virtue when it is just. "Without a 'just cause' there is no fortitude. The decisive element is not the wound but the cause," according to Pieper (1988, p.30). For hope to be a virtue it must be for directed toward "states of affairs that are morally good" (Nunn, 2004, p. 75).

The most pressing issues confronting us today are all controversial, all have a connection with the notion of justice, and all require courageous leadership. Disease, education, health care, poverty, inequality, human rights abuses, power and corruption, depletion of our natural resources, climate change, and the multiple conflicts occurring throughout the world, are *human* problems. There is adversity in everyone's life, but the greatest problems are the result of injustice more than they are the result of adversity (Kant, 1956). It is unimaginable how the participants could be compassionate and ignore injustice. According to Pieper (2003),"…anyone who judges the realities encountered in everyday life by the standard of 'justice' will clearly see that evil and suffering in our world have many names but primarily that of 'injustice'(p. 43). When the personal value of justice becomes a virtue, injustice cannot be ignored. For these leaders, personal authenticity demands they accept their freedom and responsibility to make the world more just and humane. Love demands justice.

Amynomeme fights to protect children from abuse and trauma and this action, somehow, heals her from the trauma she experienced as a child. Amos fights for the oppressed because he recognizes his burden of privilege demands no less, and he finds himself when he fulfills his obligation to speak truth to power. Athena envisions a world where people love each other in healthy community and so she commits herself to loving people and building environments that bring out the best in people. Each of these leaders has chosen to embrace the pain and suffering of others, along with the joy, hope and love. In so doing, they are healed; they become congruent, authentic, hope-filled people.

The cultivation of virtue by the participants is sustained in connection. I have chosen the word *connection* rather than the words *relationship, community* or *love* for several reasons, although any of these words could be substituted. The word love is too easily mocked and dismissed. The words relationship and community are overused in regard to all the ways we are related to each other and the universe, both constructively and destructively. Even being related by blood or marriage is no guarantee of the experience of being connected. Additionally, we may be related to someone or something without being aware of it. But when we experience a true connection, especially with another human being, it is unmistakable. To connect means "to join or fasten together" or "to establish a rapport" (Soukhanov, 1992). Connection is experienced as a communion. It is the experience of I—Thou (Buber, 1970), in which we

144

encounter life in a way not focused on utility, but with appreciation and awe. This kind of connection is a deeply meaningful experience.

Amos, Amynomeme, and Athena experience meaning and purpose through connection with others. The words love, relationship, community and connection repeatedly showed up in the data. The relationship between connection and hope was as difficult for the participants to articulate, as it is for me to elucidate. But I think Amos said it best, "You know—hope is already there [in community]. It's in the *connection* that hope is kept alive."

Limitations of the Study

This study lacks generalizability to a broad population for several reasons. First, the primary purpose of a phenomenological study is to allow the researcher to gain a deep understanding of the participants' experience, not to produce generalizable data. The study was designed to be narrow and deep with a sample size limited to three leaders of social service nonprofit organizations. They each face unique challenges. Additionally their respective organizations are distinct from nonprofits in general, and are particularly distinct from for-profit organizations (Drucker, 1990).

The study relied primarily on observation by the researcher, who shadowed each participant while they performed their professional duties. The shadowing occurred over a period of 3-4 days for each participant and was limited by the specific context and point in time during which the observation took place.

The study relied heavily on the self-report of the participants through in-depth interviews. Co-workers were not asked verify the participants' perspectives. Analysis of written documents augmented the observation and the in-depth interviews. However, individuals vary in their ability to accurately express themselves in speech and writing.

145

A limitation of this study is that it is not longitudinal. It is a snapshot in time. Therefore it is unable to show the many contextual changes that occur over time and the effect these changes have upon hope and leadership.

Finally, this study does not specifically address the technical and competency issues that are related to hope and leadership. In other words, how does the work of the organization get done? Virtue does not ensure competency in job performance. To trust an organizational leader involves trusting their judgment and ability to perform the requirements of their role in a competent manner, as well as trusting their good character. Because of these limitations, there may be other ways to do a similar study that would add more to our knowledge of the function of hope in the performance of leadership.

Recommendations for Policy

Several practical recommendations for policy may be drawn from the data. They consist of common sense practices for organizational leaders who wish to create an equitable work place, have intrinsically motivated workers, and a high level of social capital or collective efficacy—all of which contribute to a hope-filled environment. The recommendations are listed in bullet form, not necessarily in order of priority, and are a reflection of the words and behavior of the participants in this study and the policies of their organizations.

1. Be truthful; authenticity and hope depend upon it.

2. Trust people; treat them as partners and peers.

3. Never assume you know what is best for people; ask.

4. Discover the assets of the organization besides the material variety; people are more than the roles and functions they perform.

5. Clarify organizational values and make them part of your organization's performance objectives.

6. Be scrupulous about equity within your organization.

7. Do not hold onto power or exhibit a paternalistic attitude.

8. Be accountable; hold people accountable.

9. Receive advice as easily you as give it.

10. Give people the freedom to chose to the greatest extent possible.

11. Keep moving while remaining open and flexible all the time; Leadership is literally movement.

These common sense recommendations for leaders are not new. However, the widespread evidence of their absence in organizational leadership suggests that perhaps the people with the most power, hence the perceived most to lose by a change in the status quo, are not receptive to letting go of privilege. And perhaps followers may prefer not to accept their full share of freedom and accountability. Or it may be a reflection of just how difficult it is for all of us to live courageous, authentic lives.

Recommendations for Further Research

The predominant research on hope is focused on the hope of the individual and not on a socially constructed view of hope. Burns (1978) noted a serious failure in the study of leadership has been the separation between the literature on leaders and the literature on followers. The first approach often regards the leader as either a saint or demon. The second approach is based on "the conviction that in the long run, at least, leaders act as agents of their followers" (Burns, 1978, p. 3). Burns cautioned that too much emphasis on one approach over the other might be blinding. He concluded the only way to avoid the "conceptual straitjacket" (p. 31) of thinking of leadership too narrowly is to understand that first and foremost it is a relationship, a relationship with a purpose, a relationship with multiple constituencies and multiple degrees of engagement.

Leadership and hope are not things—they are *relationships*. Future research might explore the relationship between those who occupy leadership positions and those who occupy subordinate positions in organizations. Hope and the activity of leadership in the context of creating a caring community could be studied.

Future research could expand the number or participants and the type of organization. Different perspectives could be studied, for example how might younger, inexperienced leaders view hope and leadership compared with more mature, experienced leaders? More research involving Eastern cultures is needed to balance the predominance of leadership literature based on Western cultures. A longitudinal study of hope and leadership in an organization could show the effect of contextual changes. Finally, a study from within an organization that focused on hope's relationship to competency might add more to our knowledge of how hope functions in the performance of leadership.

Concluding Thoughts

When I began this study, I wanted to identify practical ways in which leaders could maximize hope within organizations by studying how hope actually functions in the performance of leadership within organizations which face challenging circumstances, like nonprofits that provide human services. I was prepared to sacrifice the ineffable beauty of hope in exchange for verifiable evidence related to how hope functions in leadership and practical suggestions for how leaders could keep hope alive. But, instead of finding a prescription for the 10 essential steps for maximizing hope in leadership, I was continually brought back to the root of hope—existential uncertainty.

In my attempt to turn hope into something that could be predicted and controlled, I was forced to make a choice. Would I ignore other dimensions of hope and focus only on the demonstrable side of hope? Hope conceptualized as goals, agency and motivation is pragmatic and easier to think, talk, and write about. Words like *practical, useful,* and *real* come to mind. Although abstract conceptualizations of hope resonated with me, incorporating this kind of hope into a study brought to mind words like *soft, sentimental,* and *illusionary*. When I first told my husband I was going to study "hope," he expressed concern that I might embarrass myself. I feared the same. But more than embarrassment, I feared I would not do justice to what I experience as critical to *everything*—that in the end I would trivialize hope.

> *World history is a cemetery of broken hopes,*
> *of utopias which had no foundation in reality.*
> —Paul Tillich

The kind of hope I had in mind was anything but trivial, was often found at the bottom, grounded in reality—face to face with our vulnerability and our possibility. When I told others I was studying hope, invariably someone would recall the popular poem by Emily Dickinson (2000) and quote dreamily, "Hope is the thing with feathers, that perches on the soul." Inwardly, I would cringe. The popularity of this poem is a testament to the fact that people often conceive of hope first and foremost as ethereal. We *need* the exquisite experience of the poetic; it is an essential dimension of the experience of hope. But hope in leadership that functions as the virtue of courage is not a flight of fancy. According to Solomon (2007), "Flight fantasies are an archetypal example of humankind's imaginative construction of supernatural conceptions of reality in response to the awareness of, and unwillingness to accept, death" (p.1).

Furthermore, Solomon claimed "hyper-individualism" is a thematic expression of the denial of death (p. 2). Real hope has no room for denial. Real hope embraces others. Real hope embraces both the tragic and exquisite realities of life.

The hope the participants have found is real. It is difficult. It requires sacrifice, courage and community. It is embodied and manifested in concrete actions and experience with persons with whom they share the pain, suffering, and tragic aspects of existence, as well as the profound love and joy of life. Ultimately, leadership and hope are not things; they are *relationships* (Burns, 1978; Marcel, 1951/96). You cannot *have* hope, not in the sense that you can have a hot dog, or a car, or any other object. Marcel claimed, "Hope is always centered on a *we*, on a living relationship and if we have not noticed this fact it is because we too often use the word hope when what is at issue is in fact [individual] desire" (1951 p. 608). He argued that hope is like a communion, no matter how interior it may be, and that the more my existence includes others, the more I am (1951, p. 58). Hope, then, functions not as the courage to merely exist, but as the courage to be *in relationship* (Tillich, 2000).

Often arguments about what is important in human life, e.g., love, hope, politics, and spirituality, go astray because we act as if facts and theories were at issue (Novak, 1978). Personal stories and experiences are viewed as subjective, while the tangible and measurable are treated as objective. But the most interesting arguments for a worldview frequently come from a sense of reality and story. Subjectivity and objectivity seem to be at war. But are they? Novak referred to claims of objectivity as "intelligent subjectivity" at best, and as "subjectivity tutored in a selected way" (p. 73).

> No matter how objective one may try to be in one's knowing, sooner or later the events of one's life ask one to choose how one will act in this or that circumstance. They ask one with relentless pressure, to declare (in action rather than words) what one most truly values, what one ultimately loves most. (p. xvi)

Actions are the real declaration of faith. As I reflected upon hope and what the actions, the stories, of Amos, Amynomeme, and Athena declare, I was again reminded of Frankl (1984) who said, "The true meaning of life is to be discovered *in* the world rather than within man or his own psyche, as though it were a closed system" (p. 115). Real hope begins by accepting one's freedom and responsibility to find meaning in life. Accepting our freedom and responsibility to choose how we respond to every circumstance in life represents a fundamental change in attitude toward life itself. While experiencing indescribable deprivation and cruelty from within a Nazi concentration camp Frankl (1984) concluded:

> It did not really matter what we expected from life, but rather what life expected from us. We needed to stop asking about the meaning of life and instead to think of ourselves as those who were being questioned by life—daily and hourly. (p. 85)

Frankl did not consider hope itself a goal, but saw it as a by-product of a meaningful life. "What is demanded of man is…not to endure the meaninglessness of life, but rather to bear his incapacity to grasp its unconditional meaningfulness in rational terms" (p. 122). Do we live in a network of meaning that transcends our pragmatic everyday lives? I did not pose this question to Amos, Amynomeme, and Athena, but their stories are evidence that they believe that we do.

REFERENCES

Argyris, C. (1993). *Knowledge for action: A guide to overcoming barriers to organizational change.* San Francisco: Jossey-Bass.

Atichison, L. (1996). Faithful wounds of an enemy: Nietzsche's "Death of God" invective." *Mars Hill Review*, Winter/Spring Issue: pp. 30-39.

Bandura, A. (1977). Self-efficacy: Toward a unifying theory of behavioral change. *Psychological Review*, Vol. 84, No. 2, pp. 191-215.

Barnard, C. (1968). *The functions of the executive.* 30th Anniversary Edition, (Original work published 1938) Cambridge, MA: Harvard University Press.

Bass, B. M. (1990). *Bass & Stogdill's handbook of leadership:Theory, research, & managerial applications.* 3rd Edition. New York: The Free Press.

Becker, E. (1973). *The denial of death.* New York: Free Press Paperbacks, a division of Simon & Schuster, Inc.

Bisesi, M. (1982). An ethic of commitment. *Contemporary Sociology*, Vol. 11, Issue 6, pp. 647-648.

Block, E. (1986). *The principle of hope.* (N. Plaice, S. Plaice, & P. Knight, Trans.) original published 1959. London: Basil Blackwell.

Block, P. (1993). *Stewardship: Choosing service over self-interest.* San Francisco: Berrett-Koehler.

Block, P. (1998). From leadership to citizenship. *Insights on Leadership: Service, Stewardship, Spirit, and Servant Leadership.* Larry Spears, Editor, New York: John Wiley & Sons.

Block, P. (2005). Keynote address, 2005 International Servant-Leadership Conference, Indianapolis, Indiana. In *The International Journal of Servant-Leadership*, Larry Spears and Shann Ferch (Eds). Vol. 2, No 1, 2006.

Boethius, A. M. S. (1962). *The consolation of philosophy.* (R. Green, Trans. for The Library of Liberal Arts), New York: The Bobbs-Merrill Company, Inc.

Bolman, L. G. & Deal, T. E. (2003). *Reframing organizations: Artistry, choice, and leadership,* 3rd Edition. San Francisco: Jossey-Bass.

Booker, C. (2004). *The seven basic plots.* New York: Continuum, ISBN: 0-8264-5209-4

Botton, Alain de, (2000). *The consolations of philosophy.* New York: Pantheon Books.

Buber, M. (1970). *I and thou.* (W. Kaufmann Trans.). New York: A Touchstone Book Published by Simon & Schuster.

Burns, J. M. (1978). *Leadership.* New York: Harper & Row Publishers.

Burns, J.M., Goethals, G.R., Sorenson, G.J., (Eds). (2004) *The encyclopedia of leadership.* Vol. 1, Thousand Oaks, CA: Sage Publications.

BusinessWeek, (2002). Special Report—The Crisis in Corporate Goverance. Retrieved on Oct, 03, 2006 from http://www.businessweek.com/magazine/content/02_18/b3278 1703.htm]

Cheavens, M., & Snyder, C. R., (2005). The correlates of hope: Psychological and physiological benefits. In J. Eliott, Ed. *Interdisciplinary perspectives on hope.* pp.119-132., Hauppauge, New York: Nova Science Publishers, Inc.

Collins, J. (2001). *Good to great: Why some companies make the leap and others don't.* New York: HarperCollins Publishers, Inc.

Collins, J. (2005). *Good to great and the social sectors: A monograph to accompany good to great.* Retrieved on Sept. 21, 2006 from www.jimcollins.com

Cousins, N. (1979). *Anatomy of an illness as perceived by the patient.* New York: Norton.

Cousins, N. (1983). *The healing heart.* New York: Norton.

Cousins, N. (1989). *Head first: The biology of hope.* New York: E.P. Dutton.

Crowley, M. (2006). Charity chislers. *Readers Digest Magazine,* Sept. '06, Prescott AZ: RDA Corp.

Csikszentmihalyi, M. (1990). *Flow: The psychology of optimal experience.* New York: Harper & Row.

Dahlberg, K., & Halling, S. (2001). Human science research as the embodiment of openness: Swimming upstream in a technological culture. *Journal of Phenomenological Psychology*, Vol. 32, No 1, 2001, pp. 12-21.

Dickinson, E. (2000). *The complete poems of Emily Dickinson.* Boston: Little, Brown, 1924; Bartleby.com, 2000. Retrieved on 09/22/05 from www.bartleby.com/113/.

Drucker, P. F. (1990). *Managing the nonprofit organization:Practices and principles.* New York: Harper Collins Publishers.

Dufault, K., & Martocchio, B.C., (1985). Hope: Its spheres and dimensions. Symposiumon compassionate care and the dying experience. *Nursing Clinics of North America*, 20(2), pp.379-391.

Dutney, Andrew (2005). Hoping for the best: Christian theology of hope in the meaner Australia. In J. Eliott (Editor), *Interdisciplinary Perspectives on Hope* (pp. 3-45). New York: Nova Science Publishers, Inc.

Dum, B.M. & Hudson, H. (2005). *Leadership in nonprofit organizations: Lessons from the third sector.* Thousand Oaks, CA: Sage Publications Inc.

Educational Directories Unlimited, (2006). GradSchools.com, Retrieved on May, 5, 2006 from http://www.gradschools.com/listings/menus/

Elbert, N. (2006). *Nonprofit executive director support.* Unpublished doctoral dissertation: Seattle University, Seattle, WA.

Eliott, J. (2005). What have we done with hope? A brief history. In J. Eliott (Ed), *Interdisciplinary Perspectives on Hope.* (pp. 3-45). New York: Nova Science Publishers, Inc.

Encyclopedia Mythica. (2007). Athena. Retrieved March 28, 2007, from http://www.pantheon.org/articles/a/athena.html

Erickson, E. (1959). *Identity and the life cycle.* International New York: University Press, Inc.

Farran, C. J., Herth, K. A., Popovich, J. M., (1995). *Hope and hopelessness: Critical clinical constructs.* Thousand Oaks, CA: Sage Publications.

Fletcher, A. (1999). The place of despair and hope. *Social Research*, Vol. 66, No. 2.

Foss, S. K. & Waters, W. (2007). *Destination dissertation: A traveler's guide to a done dissertation.* Boulder, CO: Roman & Littlefield.

Frankl, V. E. (1984). *Man's search for meaning.* (3rd ed.). New York: Simon & Schuster.

Frankl, V.E. (1988). *The will to meaning: Foundations and applications of logotherapy.* (1988 Expanded Edition) New York: First Meridian Printing.

Fromm, E. (1965). *Escape from freedom.* Avon Library Edition, 1965. New York: Holt, Rinehart & Winston.

Fromm, E. (1968). *The revolution of hope: Toward a humanized technology.* NewYork: Harper & Row, Publishers, Inc.

Gandhi, M (2006). Gandhi quotations. Retrieved on Sept. 30, 2006 from http://mindprod.com/ethics/gandhi.html#ACTION.

Gardiner, J. J. (2006). Transactional, transformational, and transcendent leadership: Metaphors mapping the evolution of the theory and practice of governance. *Leadership Review,* Vol. 6, pp. 62 –76.

Gardner, J. W. (1968). *No easy victories.* New York: Harper & Row, p. 134.

Gardner, J. W. (1982). Self-renewal: The indivdual & the innovative society. NY: W.W. Norton.

Gardner, J. W. (1987). Leaders and followers. *Liberal Education*, 73(2), pp. 4-8.

Gardner, J. W. (1990). Leadership and the future. *The Futurist*, May/June, 1990, pp. 9-12.

Gardner, J. W. (1990). *On leadership.* NY: The Free Press, A division of Simon and Schuster, Inc.

Glaser, B.G. & Strauss, A.L., (1967). *The discovery of grounded theory: Strategies for qualitative research.* New York: Aldine de Gruyter.

Godfrey, J. J. (1987). *A philosophy of human hope.* Dordrech, The Netherlands: Martinus Nijhoff

Goldsmith, M. M. (1987). *Despair: An empirical phenomenological study.* Unpublished doctoral dissertation. Duquesne University.

Gottschalk, L. A. (1974). A hope scale applicable to verbal samples. *Archives of General Psychology*, Vol. 30, pp. 779-785.

Greenleaf, R. K. (1998). *The power of servant-leadership.* (Essays by Robert K. Greenleaf, by L. C. Spears., Ed.) San Francisco, CA: Berrett-Koehler Publishers, Inc.

Groopman, J. (2004). *The anatomy of hope.* New York: Random House.

Grove, R. W. (1988). An analysis of the constant comparative method. *Qualitative Studies in Education*, Vol. 1, No. 3, pp. 273-279.

Halling, S. (2000). Meaning beyond heroic illusions? Transcendence in everyday life. *Journal of Religion and Health*, Vol. 39, No. 2, Summer 2000, pp. 143-156.

Halling, S. (2002). Making Phenomenology Accessible to a wider audience. *Journal of Phenomenological Psychology*, 33:1

Harter, N. (2006). *Clearings in the forest: On the study of leadership.* West LaFayette, IN: Purdue University Press.

Havel, V. (1993). Never against hope. *Esquire*. October, 1993, pp. 65-69.

Heifetz, R. A. (1994). *Leadership without easy answers.* Cambridge, MA: The Belknap Press of Harvard University Press.

Heifetz, R. A., & Linsky, M. (2002). *Leadership on the line: Staying alive through the dangers of leading.* Boston:Harvard Business School Press.

Herman, R. D. (2005). *The Jossey-Bass handbook of nonprofit leadership & mangagement.* Second Ed., San Francisco: Jossey-Bass.

Herman, R. D. & Heimovics, D. (2005). Executive leadership. *The Jossey-Bass handbook of nonprofit leadership & mangagement.* 2nd Ed., (Herman, R. D., Eds.) San Francisco, CA: Jossey-Bass.

Homer, (1993). *The Odyssey.* Translation by Samuel Butler. New York: Barnes & Noble Books, Publisher.

Hope News. (2006). *Hope news.* Summer Issue 2006. Alberta, Canada: The Hope Foundation of Alberta.

Independent Sector, (2006). Charitable fact sheet. Retrieved Nov 30, 2006 from http://www.independentsector.org/programs/research/

Jaffee, M. (2002). Fessing up in theory. [electronic version] *Theory & Method in the Study of Religion: Theoretical and Critical Readings.* Ed. Carl Olson. Wadsworth Publisher. 2002. p. 2. http://jsis.artsci.washington.edu/programs/relig/jaffee_pub1.html

James, W. (1890). The principles of psychology. [electronic version] *Classics in the History of Psychology.* An internet resource developed by Christopher D. Green. York Unversity, Toronto, Ontario. Harvard University, August 1890.

James, W. (2005). *William James Talks to Teachers on Psychology.* Retrieved on August 18, 2005 from http://www.des.emory.edu/mfp/talksto.html

Jeavons, T. H. (2005). Ethical nonprofit management. *The Jossey-Bass Handbook of Nonprofit Leadership & Mangagement.* 2nd Ed., (Herman, R. D., Editor) San Francisco, CA: Jossey-Bass.

Jenks, P. (2006). *Congressional scandals, corruption and misbehavior.* Retrieved on Oct. 16, 2006, from http://www.llrx.com/congress/scandals.html

Jevne, R. F. (1994). *The voice of hope: Heard across the heart of a life.* San Diego, CA: Lura Media Publishers.

Jevne, R.F. (2005). Hope: The Simplicity and Complexity. In J. Eliott (Editor), *Interdisciplinary Perspectives on Hope* (pp. 3-45). New York: Nova Science Publishers, Inc.

Jevne, R. F. (2005). Hope and justice. *Hope News,* Edmonton, AB: a publication of the Hope Foundation of Alberta. Fall Issue.

Kant, I. (1950). *The critique of pure reason.* (Translated by Norman Kemp Smith) London: MacMillan and Co.

Kant, I. (1956). *Groundwork of the metaphysic of morals.* (Translated by H.J. Paton) New York: Harper and Row, Publishers.

Kaufmann, W. (1968). *Basic writings of Nietzsche*. First ModernLibrary Edition.,
     New York: Random House Inc.

Kaufmann, W. (1989). *Existentialism from Dostroevsky to Sartre*. New York:
     A Meridian book published by the Penguin Group

Kellerman, B. (2004). *Bad leadership: What it is, how it happens, why it matters*. Boston:
     Harvard Business School Press.

Kierkegaard, S. (1980). *The sickness unto death*. (V. Hong & E.H. Hong, Eds, & Trans)
     Princeton: Princeton University Press.

Knowledge@Wharton, (2006). CEO pay: A window into corporate governance, May 17,
     2006. Retrieved on Oct. 3, 2006 from
     http://knowledge.wharton.upenn.edu/article.cfm?articleid=1481&CFID=1322812&C
     FTOKEN=34903470].

Koestenbaum, P., & Block, P. (2001). *Freedom and accountability at work: Applying
     philosophic insight to the real world*. San Francisco: Jossey-Bass/Pfeiffer,
     A Wiley Company.

Kouzes, J., & Posner, B. (2002). *The leadership challenge*. 3rd Edition, San Francisco:
     Jossey-Bass.

Lager, F. (1994). *Ben & Jerry's: The inside scoop: How two real guys built a business with
     a social conscience and a sense of humor*. New York: Random House.

Lane, D. A. (1996). *Keeping hope alive: Stirrings in Christian theology*. Mahwah,
     New Jersey: Paulist Press.

Lanchester, J. (2006). Pursuing happiness: Two scholars explore the fragility of contentment.
     The New Yorker, Issue 2006-02-27.

Larsen, D., Edey, W., & LeMay, L.M. (2005). Put hope to work. *Journal of Advanced
     Nursing*. Vol. 52., Issue 5, p. 515. December, 2005.

Lewis, Charles. (1992). Making sense of common sense. *Critical Studies in Mass
     Communication*. September 1992, pp. 277-92.

Lincoln, Y. & Guba, E. (1985). *Naturalistic inquiry*. New York: Sage Publications, Inc.

Lipman-Blumen, J. (2005). *The allure of toxic leader: Why we follow destructive bosses and
     corrupt politicians—and how we can survive them*. New York & Oxford:
     Oxford University Press.

Lazarus, R. (1999). Hope: An emotion and vital coping resource against despair.
     Social Research, Vol. 66, No. 2.

Lynch, W., F. (S.J.) (1965). *Images of hope: Imagination as healer of the hopeless.* Baltimore: Helicon Press, Inc.

Marcel, G. (1962). *Homo viator: An introduction to the metaphysic of hope.* (Emma Craufurd Trans.) New York: Harper & Row, Publishers. (Originally published in English by Victor Gollancz, Ltd., London, 1951.)

Marcel, G. (1996). The structure of hope. *Communio.* Vol 23, p 604. Translated by David-Louis Schindler, Jr. from Gabriel Marcel, "Structure de l'esperance" in *Dieu vivant:perspectives, religieuse et philosophiques.* (Original work published in 1951)

McConnon, T. (1959). *Angles in Hell's Kitchen.* New York: Double Day.

McDermott, D., & Snyder, C.R. (2000). *Making hope happen.* Oakland, CA: New Harbinger Publications.

McLean, B. & Elkind, P. (2003). *The smartest guys in the room: The amazing rise and scandalous fall of Enron.* New York: Penguin (USA) Group.

Murphy, J.T. (1980). *Getting the facts: the fieldwork guide forevaluators and policy analysts.* Santa Monica, CA: Goodyear.

Nelson, J.A. (1982). *Hunger for Justice: The Politics of Food and Faith.* New York: Orbis Books.

Niebuhr, R., (1892-1971). Wilkipedia. Retrieved on 05/30/06 from http://en.wikipedia.org/wiki/Serenity_Prayer#_note-0

Nietzsche(1840/1900). Wikiquote. Retrieved on 05/05/05 http://en.wikiquote.org/wiki/Human,_All_Too_Human

Nietzsche, F. (1982). *Nietzschez: Thus spoke zarathustra.* (W. Kaufmann Trans., & Prologue.). New York: Published by Penguin Books.

Novak, Michael. (1978). *Ascent of the mountain, flight of the dove.* New York: Harper & Row, Publishers.

Nunn, B.V. (2004). Getting clear what hope is. In J. Eliott (Ed) *Interdisciplinary Perspectives on Hope.* (pp. 63-77). New York: Nova Science Publishers, Inc.

Parse, R. R. (1999). *Hope: An international human becoming perspective.* R. R. Parse, Editor., Sudbury, MA: Jones and Bartlett Publishers.

Peña, R. A. (2005). Water is clear like me: A story about race, identity, teaching, and social justice. *Community and Difference: Teaching, Pluralism, and Social Justice.* R.A Peña, K. Guest & L. Y. Matsuda, Editors. New York: Peter Lang.

Pieper, J. (1969). *Hope and history.* New York: Herder and Herder.

Pieper. J. (1988). *A brief reader on the virtues of the human heart.* San Francisco. CA: Ignatius Press.

Pieper, J. (1997). *Faith-hope-love.* San Francisco. CA: Ignatius Press.

Pilkington, (1999). The many facets of hope. *Hope: An International Human Becoming Perspective.* Editor: R. R. Parse, Editor., Sudbury, MA: Jones and Bartlett Publishers.

Porter, L.W., Bigley, G. A., & Steers, R. M. (2003) *Motivation and work behavior.* 7th Edition., New York: McGraw-Hill Companies, Inc,

Quoteworld, (2006). Reinhold Niebuhr. Retrieved on Oct. 5, 2006 from http://www.quoteworld.org/quotes/9391

Radich, A. J. (1986). *Governance in nonprofit arts organizations: A grounded theory perspective.* Unpublished doctoral dissertation, University of Colorado.

Ryan, R. M., & Deci, E. L. (2004). Avoiding death or engaging life as accounts of meaning and culture. *Psychological Bulletin,* Vol. 130, No. 3, pp. 473-477.

Roset, S.M. (2004). *Images of hope: How leaders conceptualize, experience,and seek to foster hope.* Unpublished doctoral dissertation. University of Saskatchewan

Ruffell, J. (1997). *Brave women warriors of Greek mythology.* Retrieved on Mar. 1, 2007 from http://whoosh.org/issue12/ruffel3.html

Seligman, M. & Csikszentmihalyi, M. (2000). Positive Psychology: An introduction. *American Psychologist,* 55 (1), 5-14.

Seligman, M. (1990). *Learned optimism: How to change your mind and your life.* New York: The Free Press, a division of Simon & Schuster, Inc.

Seligman, M. (2002). *Authentic happiness: Using the new positive psychology to realize your potential for lasting fulfillment.* New York: The Free Press, a division of Simon & Schuster, Inc.

Shade, P. (2001). *Habits of hope: A pragmatic theory.* Nashville, TN: Vanderbilt University Press.

Smith, J. (2005). *Swimming against the tide: On being a qualitative psychologist.* Unpublished lecture given at Seattle University, Seattle, WA. on July 19, 2005.

Snyder, C. R., Higgins, R. L., & Stucky, R. J. (1983). *Excuses: Masquerades in search of grace.* New York: John Wiley & Sons.

Snyder, C.R. (1994). *The psychology of hope: You can get there from here.* New York: The Free Press.

Snyder, C.R., McDermott, D., Cook, W., Rapoff, M. A. (1997). *Hope for the journey: Helping children through good times and bad.* Boulder, Colorado: Westview Press, a division of HarperCollins.

Snyder, C.R. (1999) Coping: The psychology of what works. C.R. Snyder (Ed), New York & Oxford: Oxford University Press.

Snyder, C. R. (2000a). *Handbook of hope: Theory, Measures, and Applications.* C.R. Snyder Editor., San Diego, CA: Academic Press, a Harcourt Science & Technology Co.

Snyder, C.R. (2000b). The past and possible futures of hope. *Journal of Social and Clinical Psychology.* New York: Spring 2000, Vol. 19, Issue 1.

Snyder, C.R. (2002). Hope Theory: Rainbows of the mind. *Psychological Inquiry,* 13 249-275.

Snyder, C.R., & Rand, K. L. (2003). The case against false hope. *American Psychologist,* October, Vol, 58, No. 10, pp. 820-822.

Snyder, C.R., Cheavens, J.S. & Michael, S.T. (2005). Hope theory: History and elaborated model. In Eliott, J. (Ed.), *Interdisciplinary Perspectives on Hope.* NY: Nova Science Publishers, Inc.

Solomon, S. (2007). Teach these souls to fly: The psychology of supernatural belief. *The Ernest Becker Foundation Newsletter.* Vol. 14, Number 2, April, 2007.

Soukhanov, A. H. (Ed.). (1992). *The American Heritage Dictionary of the English Language,* 3rd Edition. New York: Houghton Mifflin Co.

Stacks, D.W. & Hocking, J.E. (1999). *Communication Research,* 2nd Edition. New York: Longman by Addison-Wesley Educational Publishers, Inc.

Stewart, M. (2005). "Prometheus", *Greek Mythology: From the Iliad to the Fall of the Last Tyrant.* Retrieved on June 5, 2005 from http://messagenet.com/myths/bios/promethe.html

Stotland, Ezra (1969). *The psychology of hope.* San Francisco, CA: Jossey-Bass.

Taylor, S.J. and Bogdan, R. (1998). *Introduction to qualitative research methods: A guidebook and resource.* 3rd Edition. New York: John Wiley & Sons, Inc.

Terence (195-159 BC). Brainyquote. Retrieval on Sept. 22, 2006 from http://www.brainyquote.com/quotes/authors/t/terence.html

The Hope Foundation of Alberta. (2006). Retrieved on Sept. 18, 2006 from http://www.ualberta.ca/HOPE/

Tillich, P. (2000). *The courage to be.* 2nd Edition. New Haven & London: Yale University Press.

Tomlin, L. (2006). The quotations page. Retrieved on August 22, 2006 from
http://www.quotationspage.com/subjects/cynicism/

Yankelovich, D. (2003). *A matter of trust*. Retrieval on Oct. 16, 2006 from
http://www.danyankelovich.com/matteroftrust.pdf

Yukl, G. A. (2002). *Leadership in organizations.* 5th Edition. Upper Saddle River,
New Jersey: Prentice-Hall.

Wissenschaftlicher Buchverlag bietet

kostenfreie

Publikation

von

wissenschaftlichen Arbeiten

Diplomarbeiten, Magisterarbeiten, Master und Bachelor Theses
sowie Dissertationen, Habilitationen und wissenschaftliche Monographien

Sie verfügen über eine wissenschaftliche Abschlußarbeit zu aktuellen oder zeitlosen
Fragestellungen, die hohen inhaltlichen und formalen Ansprüchen genügt,
und haben **Interesse an einer honorarvergüteten Publikation**?

Dann senden Sie bitte erste Informationen über Ihre Arbeit per Email
an info@vdm-verlag.de. Unser Außenlektorat meldet sich umgehend bei Ihnen.

VDM Verlag Dr. Müller Aktiengesellschaft & Co. KG
Dudweiler Landstraße 125a
D - 66123 Saarbrücken

www.vdm-verlag.de

Printed in the United States
137170LV00004B/3/P